mtG

NCO OLYMPIAD WORKBOOK 9

SOF NATIONAL CYBER OLYMPIAD 2018-19

By
Meetu Misra

MTG Learning Media (P) Ltd.
New Delhi | Gurgaon

Corporate Office : Plot 99, Sector 44 Institutional area, Gurgaon -122 003 (HR) Telefax: 0124-6601200
Regd. Office : 406, Taj Apt., Ring Road, Adjacent Safdarjung Hospital, New Delhi - 110 029.
Web: mtg.in Email: info@mtg.in

CONTENTS

Page No.

* *Based on Windows 7 and MS-Office 2010*

SAMPLE OMR ANSWER SHEET

1. STUDENT NAME (IN ENGLISH CAPITAL LETTERS ONLY)

IMPORTANT: *PLEASE FILL IN SCHOOL CODE, CLASS, SECTION & ROLL NO. CORRECTLY FOR COMPUTATION OF RESULT.*

PERSONAL DETAILS

2. SCHOOL CODE

Ⓐ–Ⓩ | Ⓐ–Ⓩ | 0–9 | 0–9 | 0–9 | 0–9

3. CLASS

0–1 | 0–9

4. SECTION

A B C D E F G H I J K L M N O P Q R S T U V W X Y Z

5. ROLL NO.

0–9 | 0–9 | 0–9

6. QUESTION PAPER SET

A ○ B ○ C ○ D ○

** Result of the Olympiad and other information may be sent to you through SMS at the following No.*

7. MOBILE NUMBER

(Write your Mobile no. in the boxes and darken the circles)

0–9 (10 columns)

8. GENDER

MALE ○

FEMALE ○

USE HB PENCIL

OR

USE BLUE/BLACK BALL POINT PEN

MARK YOUR ANSWERS

1.	Ⓐ	Ⓑ	Ⓒ	Ⓓ	26.	Ⓐ	Ⓑ	Ⓒ	Ⓓ
2.	Ⓐ	Ⓑ	Ⓒ	Ⓓ	27.	Ⓐ	Ⓑ	Ⓒ	Ⓓ
3.	Ⓐ	Ⓑ	Ⓒ	Ⓓ	28.	Ⓐ	Ⓑ	Ⓒ	Ⓓ
4.	Ⓐ	Ⓑ	Ⓒ	Ⓓ	29.	Ⓐ	Ⓑ	Ⓒ	Ⓓ
5.	Ⓐ	Ⓑ	Ⓒ	Ⓓ	30.	Ⓐ	Ⓑ	Ⓒ	Ⓓ
6.	Ⓐ	Ⓑ	Ⓒ	Ⓓ	31.	Ⓐ	Ⓑ	Ⓒ	Ⓓ
7.	Ⓐ	Ⓑ	Ⓒ	Ⓓ	32.	Ⓐ	Ⓑ	Ⓒ	Ⓓ
8.	Ⓐ	Ⓑ	Ⓒ	Ⓓ	33.	Ⓐ	Ⓑ	Ⓒ	Ⓓ
9.	Ⓐ	Ⓑ	Ⓒ	Ⓓ	34.	Ⓐ	Ⓑ	Ⓒ	Ⓓ
10.	Ⓐ	Ⓑ	Ⓒ	Ⓓ	35.	Ⓐ	Ⓑ	Ⓒ	Ⓓ
11.	Ⓐ	Ⓑ	Ⓒ	Ⓓ					
12.	Ⓐ	Ⓑ	Ⓒ	Ⓓ					

THIS COLUMN IS FOR CLASSES 5 & ABOVE

13.	Ⓐ	Ⓑ	Ⓒ	Ⓓ	36.	Ⓐ	Ⓑ	Ⓒ	Ⓓ
14.	Ⓐ	Ⓑ	Ⓒ	Ⓓ	37.	Ⓐ	Ⓑ	Ⓒ	Ⓓ
15.	Ⓐ	Ⓑ	Ⓒ	Ⓓ	38.	Ⓐ	Ⓑ	Ⓒ	Ⓓ
16.	Ⓐ	Ⓑ	Ⓒ	Ⓓ	39.	Ⓐ	Ⓑ	Ⓒ	Ⓓ
17.	Ⓐ	Ⓑ	Ⓒ	Ⓓ	40.	Ⓐ	Ⓑ	Ⓒ	Ⓓ
18.	Ⓐ	Ⓑ	Ⓒ	Ⓓ	41.	Ⓐ	Ⓑ	Ⓒ	Ⓓ
19.	Ⓐ	Ⓑ	Ⓒ	Ⓓ	42.	Ⓐ	Ⓑ	Ⓒ	Ⓓ
20.	Ⓐ	Ⓑ	Ⓒ	Ⓓ	43.	Ⓐ	Ⓑ	Ⓒ	Ⓓ
21.	Ⓐ	Ⓑ	Ⓒ	Ⓓ	44.	Ⓐ	Ⓑ	Ⓒ	Ⓓ
22.	Ⓐ	Ⓑ	Ⓒ	Ⓓ	45.	Ⓐ	Ⓑ	Ⓒ	Ⓓ
23.	Ⓐ	Ⓑ	Ⓒ	Ⓓ	46.	Ⓐ	Ⓑ	Ⓒ	Ⓓ
24.	Ⓐ	Ⓑ	Ⓒ	Ⓓ	47.	Ⓐ	Ⓑ	Ⓒ	Ⓓ
25.	Ⓐ	Ⓑ	Ⓒ	Ⓓ	48.	Ⓐ	Ⓑ	Ⓒ	Ⓓ
					49.	Ⓐ	Ⓑ	Ⓒ	Ⓓ
					50.	Ⓐ	Ⓑ	Ⓒ	Ⓓ

Signature of the Student & Date of Examination

Signature of the Invigilator & Date of Examination

CHAPTER 1

FUNDAMENTALS OF COMPUTER

[This chapter covers questions on Hardware, Software, Input/Output Devices, Operating System, Memory and Storage Devices]

1. A ________ is a small but high speed storage area found in most modern CPUs.
   (A) Instruction set
   (B) Address Bus
   (C) Processor Register
   (D) Printed Circuit Board

2. Identify the following:
   – It acts as a central nervous system for other components of computer.
   – It manages and coordinates entire computer system.
   – It obtains instructions from a program stored in main memory, interprets instructions and issues signals that cause other units of system to execute them.
   (A) ALU
   (B) Memory Register
   (C) Control Unit
   (D) ROM

3. A computer's clock cycle is used to measure ________ .
   (A) The ratio of accuracy of its internal clock to an external clock
   (B) The CPU's processing speed
   (C) The amount of time taken by the computer to read information from its internal memory
   (D) Accuracy of system clock

4. Shreya is using an operating system that allows her to click and drag objects with mouse instead of entering commands. Which type of operating system she might be using?
   (A) GUI (B) CLI
   (C) SSI (D) DSI

5. A/An ________ is the single transaction between the system memory and the CPU.
   (A) Bus cycle (B) Bit node
   (C) Data unit (D) I/O cycle

6. Which of the following hardware device is used for controlling unmanned vehicles, cranes, etc and is also called as control column?

(A) 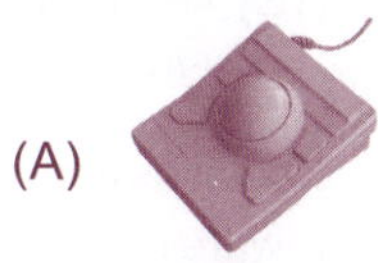  (B) 

(C)   (D)  

7. Which of the following statements hold(s) true about 'SDIO' card?

Statement 1: It enables devices to use SD slot to support bluetooth adapters, GPS receivers, digital cameras, barcode readers, etc.

Statement 2: It is DRAM based volatile memory card.

(A) Only Statement 1
(B) Only Statement 2
(C) Both Statement 1 and Statement 2
(D) Neither Statement 1 nor Statement 2

8. A CMOS can maintain its configuration settings due to ________ present on motherboard.

(A) The BIOS
(B) The system board
(C) The power supply
(D) The battery

9. Your computer is showing incorrect time every time you start it. This happens even after you have set the computer time several times. What needs to be done?

(A) The CPU needs to be replaced.
(B) The UPS needs to be replaced.
(C) The CMOS battery needs to be replaced.
(D) The operating system must be reloaded.

10. Which of the following memory can be used for firmware in automatic appliances.

(A) ROM (B) PROM
(C) EPROM (D) All of these

11. It is a computer bus which moves information between the internal hardware of a computer system (including the CPU and RAM) and peripheral devices.

(A) Information Bus
(B) Descend Bus
(C) Ascend Bus
(D) Expansion Bus

12. ________ is NOT a type of internal hard drive.

(A) IDE (B) SCSI
(C) USB (D) EIDE

13. Flash CS6 is an example of ________ software.

(A) Multimedia
(B) Utility
(C) Presentation
(D) Specific Purpose Application

14. Which of the following operations are NOT performed by system software?

(A) Reading data from input devices.
(B) Converting data and instructions in binary form – making it easily understandable by the computer.
(C) Creating a logo for the system software that is being used on the computer.
(D) Checking the working of all peripheral devices.

15. Which of the following statements is CORRECT about ERP systems?

(A) It is a business management software.
(B) It integrates several application of a company to collect data from different activities like manufacturing, marketing, sales, etc.
(C) It falls under the category of processor software.
(D) Both (A) and (B)

16. A light pen ________ .

(A) Can draw directly on screen
(B) Is cheaper than mouse
(C) Can be used for long hours without any fatigue
(D) Is always accurate while drawing

17. Special encoding schemes are used to ________ files using fewer bits of data than the original to reduce disk space.
(A) Decode
(B) Compress
(C) Scatter
(D) Fragment

18. Concentric circles on the magnetic surface of the magnetic disks are known as ________ . The track on the disk surface are divided into invisible segments known as ________ .
(A) Tracks, Sector
(B) Platters, Actuator
(C) Spots, Arms
(D) Actuator, Spots

19. ________ storage technology is used to store the information on cheques and credit/debit cards.
(A) Optical
(B) Laser
(C) Magnetic
(D) None of these

20. Find the odd one out.
(A) QuickTime™
(B)
(C) debian
(D) Office

21. __________ is closely associated with computer related crimes.
(A) Word processing software
(B) Malicious software
(C) Crimious software
(D) Cruel software

22. _________ is a type of 2D barcode, consisting of an array of black and white squares.
(A) Smart code
(B) Square code
(C) Bubble code
(D) QR code

23. A software is called robust, if __________
(A) It can cope up data errors.
(B) It is authorized to specific users.
(C) It can be used to control system performance.
(D) It is written in low level language.

24. Which of the following statements is CORRECT about the given logo?
(A) It provides basic functionality to the computer.
(B) It converts a high level language program into machine language.
(C) It is designed to operate computer hardware.
(D) None of these

25. ________ operating system works on specified time constraint.
(A) Distributed
(B) Real-time
(C) Single-user
(D) Appropriate

26. _________ is/are example(s) of utility software.
(A) Disk Defragmenter
(B) Antivirus Software
(C) Backup Utility
(D) All of these

27. Which of the following printers CANNOT be used to print high quality graphics?
(A) Daisy wheel printer
(B) LED printer

(C) Inkjet printer
(D) Laser printer

28. Toner is a powder used to form the printed text and images on the paper. Which of the following is an example of toner-based printer?
(A) Inkjet printer
(B) Thermal printer
(C) Laser printer
(D) Dot-matrix printer

29. Which of the following printer uses photocopy technology to print?
(A) Inkjet printer
(B) Laser printer
(C) Dot matrix printer
(D) All of these

30. Which of the following scanners has a glass window where the document/object is placed for scanning?
(A) Drum scanner
(B) Flatbed scanner
(C) Hand held scanner
(D) All of these

Achievers Section (HOTS)

31. Observe the given diagram and identify which of the following system software is making the high level language program understandable to computer?

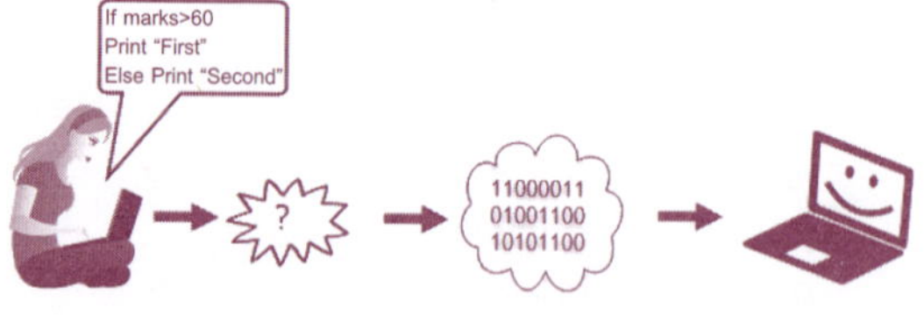

(A) Operating System
(B) Language Processor
(C) Device Driver
(D) Disk Archiver

32. Which of the following statements is INCORRECT about SIMM?
(A) It is a small circuit board.
(B) It can hold a group of memory chips.
(C) SIMM stands for single in-line memory module.
(D) It is a sequential access memory used in early computers.

33. Which of the following statements is CORRECT about the given device?

(i) It has slower data rate than internally mounted hard drives.
(ii) Its storage capacity ranges from 160 GB to 6 TB.
(iii) It uses an interface called EDE.
(A) Only (i)
(B) Both (i) and (ii)
(C) Both (ii) and (iii)
(D) All (i), (ii) and (iii)

34. AIDC refers to the methods of automatically identifying objects, collect data about them and entering that data directly into computer systems without human involvement.
AIDC stands for ________ .
(A) Automatic Input by Data Capture
(B) Automatic Identification and Data Capture
(C) Automatic Identification by Device Computer
(D) Automatic Identity of Data Converted

35. ICR is one of the technologies used for collecting information from paper documents and saving it into databases. ICR is used for ________ .

(A) Printed text recognition
(B) Marks recognition
(C) Handwriting recognition
(D) Business cards recognition

Darken your choice with HB Pencil

1.	Ⓐ	Ⓑ	Ⓒ	Ⓓ	11.	Ⓐ	Ⓑ	Ⓒ	Ⓓ	21.	Ⓐ	Ⓑ	Ⓒ	Ⓓ	31.	Ⓐ	Ⓑ	Ⓒ	Ⓓ
2.	Ⓐ	Ⓑ	Ⓒ	Ⓓ	12.	Ⓐ	Ⓑ	Ⓒ	Ⓓ	22.	Ⓐ	Ⓑ	Ⓒ	Ⓓ	32.	Ⓐ	Ⓑ	Ⓒ	Ⓓ
3.	Ⓐ	Ⓑ	Ⓒ	Ⓓ	13.	Ⓐ	Ⓑ	Ⓒ	Ⓓ	23.	Ⓐ	Ⓑ	Ⓒ	Ⓓ	33.	Ⓐ	Ⓑ	Ⓒ	Ⓓ
4.	Ⓐ	Ⓑ	Ⓒ	Ⓓ	14.	Ⓐ	Ⓑ	Ⓒ	Ⓓ	24.	Ⓐ	Ⓑ	Ⓒ	Ⓓ	34.	Ⓐ	Ⓑ	Ⓒ	Ⓓ
5.	Ⓐ	Ⓑ	Ⓒ	Ⓓ	15.	Ⓐ	Ⓑ	Ⓒ	Ⓓ	25.	Ⓐ	Ⓑ	Ⓒ	Ⓓ	35.	Ⓐ	Ⓑ	Ⓒ	Ⓓ
6.	Ⓐ	Ⓑ	Ⓒ	Ⓓ	16.	Ⓐ	Ⓑ	Ⓒ	Ⓓ	26.	Ⓐ	Ⓑ	Ⓒ	Ⓓ					
7.	Ⓐ	Ⓑ	Ⓒ	Ⓓ	17.	Ⓐ	Ⓑ	Ⓒ	Ⓓ	27.	Ⓐ	Ⓑ	Ⓒ	Ⓓ					
8.	Ⓐ	Ⓑ	Ⓒ	Ⓓ	18.	Ⓐ	Ⓑ	Ⓒ	Ⓓ	28.	Ⓐ	Ⓑ	Ⓒ	Ⓓ					
9.	Ⓐ	Ⓑ	Ⓒ	Ⓓ	19.	Ⓐ	Ⓑ	Ⓒ	Ⓓ	29.	Ⓐ	Ⓑ	Ⓒ	Ⓓ					
10.	Ⓐ	Ⓑ	Ⓒ	Ⓓ	20.	Ⓐ	Ⓑ	Ⓒ	Ⓓ	30.	Ⓐ	Ⓑ	Ⓒ	Ⓓ					

CHAPTER 2

ALGORITHMS AND FLOWCHARTS IN PROGRAMMING

1. A ________ is a type of diagram that represents an algorithm or process by showing the steps as boxes of different types in a particular sequence connected with directional arrows.
   (A) Pie chart (B) Flowchart
   (C) Algorithm (D) Data chart

2. The efficiency of an algorithm in terms of its memory requirements is measured by ________ .
   (A) The maximum memory needed by the algorithm
   (B) The minimum memory needed by the algorithm
   (C) The primary memory needed to load the algorithm
   (D) The maximum disk space needed by the algorithm

3. For which of the purpose a parallelogram is used in a flowchart?
   (A) To denote the step in which data is stored.
   (B) To denote a step in which decision has to be made.
   (C) To show a step that cannot be resolved.
   (D) To show input or output.

4. The following statements are examples of ________.
   COUNT = 20
   SUM = SUM + COUNT
   COUNT = COUNT + 1
   (A) Assignment statements
   (B) Declaration statements
   (C) Input statements
   (D) Output statements

5. To allow operations to be repeated a fixed number of time or until some condition is met, we use the __________ structure.
   (A) Selection (B) Loop
   (C) Sequential (D) Simple

6. It is a program planning tool allowing programmers to plan program logic by writing program instructions in a language like english, which can be easily converted into real programming statements without using symbols. Identify it.
   (A) Pseudocode
   (B) Flowchart
   (C) High level program
   (D) Assembly language program

7. Which of the following symbols indicates a subroutine/procedure that is completely described in a separate flowchart segment?
   (A) [rectangle with double vertical side lines] (B) [hexagon]
   (C) [cylinder] (D) [diamond]

8. A flowchart using symbols displays the ________ to be performed and the ________ in which they occur.

(A) Sequence, program
(B) Decisions, flow
(C) Operations, sequence
(D) Program, operations

9. The symbol displayed in the given flowchart is called a/an ________.

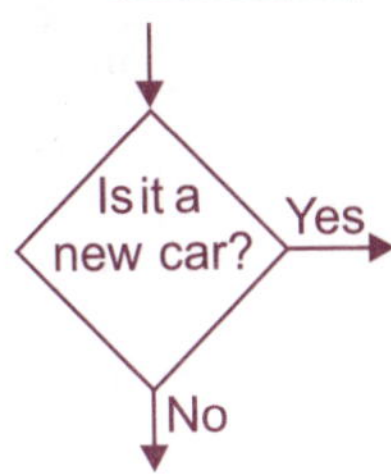

(A) On page connector
(B) Off page connector
(C) Terminal symbol
(D) Decision symbol

10. Which of the following statements hold(s) true about manually drawn flowchart?
Statement 1 : They provide better communication because even the non-programmers can understand the logic of program.
Statement 2 : They can be modified frequently as per the requirement if there is any change.
(A) Only Statement 1
(B) Only Statement 2
(C) Both Statement 1 and Statement 2
(D) Neither Statement 1 nor Statement 2

11. The arrows displayed here is used for __________ in a flowchart.

(A) Representing direction and sequence of processes.
(B) Asking questions and then determines which route the program will take
(C) Representing input into the program or output from the program
(D) Representing an action taken by the program.

12. Which of the following statements is INCORRECT in case of a flowchart?
(A) Program flowcharts serves as a good program documentation and can be used for various purposes.
(B) Maintaining and operating program becomes easy with a flowchart. It helps the programmer to put efforts more efficiently.
(C) Any symbol can be used as a part of the flowchart – as desired by the creator of the flowchart.
(D) Flowcharts acts as a reference during system analysis and program development phase.

13. While writing an algorithm, instructions are written from __________ .
(A) Top to Bottom
(B) Left to Right
(C) Right to Left
(D) It depends on the author of the algorithm

14. An algorithm is ___________ .
(A) Collection of symbols used to design a flowchart
(B) A self contained step-by-step set of operations to be performed in the given sequence
(C) A set of instruction to be followed before choosing a programming language.
(D) A help guide that instructs how to use a software.

15. Jayant is drawing a flowchart in which he has to show a step which needs to be calculated manually. Which of the following shapes will he select for that step?

(A)
(B)
(C)
(D)

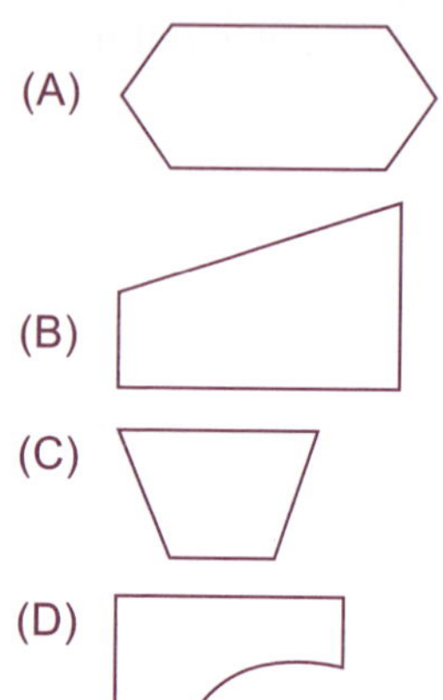

Achievers Section (HOTS)

16. Given here is an algorithm to swap two numbers. Which of the following line will replace "?" to complete the algorithm?

    Step 1: Read two numbers X and Y.
    Step 2: ?
    Step 3: Y = X – Y
    Step 4: X = X – Y

    (A) X = X + Y
    (B) X = X × Y
    (C) X = X/Y
    (D) X = X – Y

17. What would be the result upon executing the steps shown in the given flowchart. if 4 is entered for P?

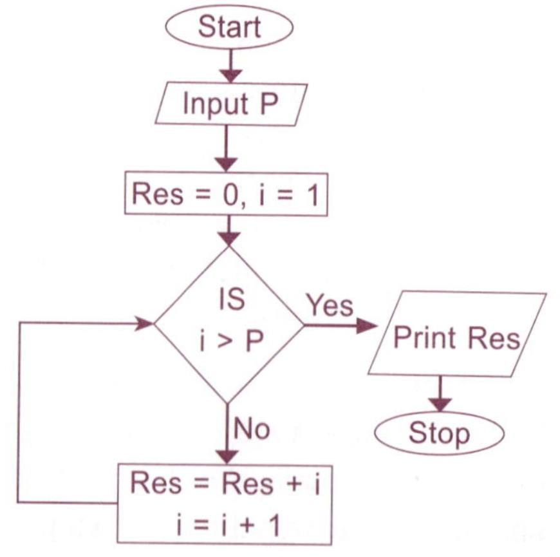

(A) 6
(B) 10
(C) 8
(D) 12

18. If N = 5, then the output generated by the given flowchart is ________.

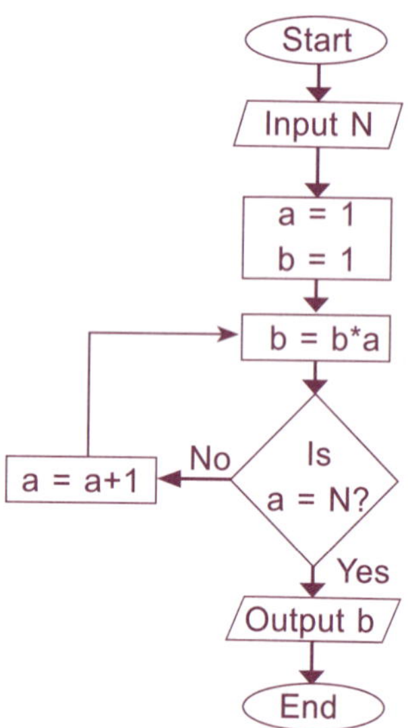

(A) Product of three numbers
(B) Sum of three numbers
(C) Table of 5
(D) None of these

19. Predict the output of the given flowchart.

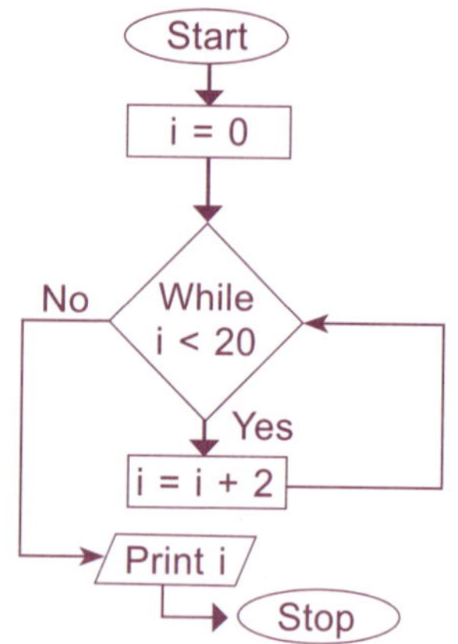

(A) 18
(B) 20
(C) 22
(D) Loop will run infinitely

20. The given flowchart has been drawn to calculate the area of rectangle. But, for one of the steps an incorrect shape is used. Identify it.

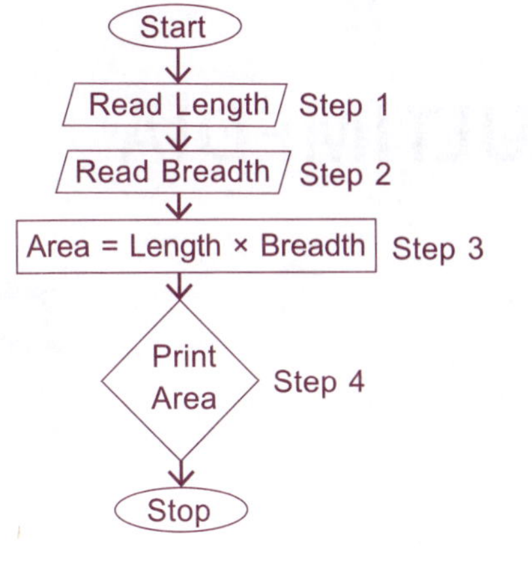

(A) Step 1
(B) Step 2
(C) Step 3
(D) Step 4

☺☺☺

Darken your choice with HB Pencil

1.	Ⓐ Ⓑ Ⓒ Ⓓ	7.	Ⓐ Ⓑ Ⓒ Ⓓ	13.	Ⓐ Ⓑ Ⓒ Ⓓ	19.	Ⓐ Ⓑ Ⓒ Ⓓ
2.	Ⓐ Ⓑ Ⓒ Ⓓ	8.	Ⓐ Ⓑ Ⓒ Ⓓ	14.	Ⓐ Ⓑ Ⓒ Ⓓ	20.	Ⓐ Ⓑ Ⓒ Ⓓ
3.	Ⓐ Ⓑ Ⓒ Ⓓ	9.	Ⓐ Ⓑ Ⓒ Ⓓ	15.	Ⓐ Ⓑ Ⓒ Ⓓ		
4.	Ⓐ Ⓑ Ⓒ Ⓓ	10.	Ⓐ Ⓑ Ⓒ Ⓓ	16.	Ⓐ Ⓑ Ⓒ Ⓓ		
5.	Ⓐ Ⓑ Ⓒ Ⓓ	11.	Ⓐ Ⓑ Ⓒ Ⓓ	17.	Ⓐ Ⓑ Ⓒ Ⓓ		
6.	Ⓐ Ⓑ Ⓒ Ⓓ	12.	Ⓐ Ⓑ Ⓒ Ⓓ	18.	Ⓐ Ⓑ Ⓒ Ⓓ		

CHAPTER

3

ANIMATIONS & MULTIMEDIA

1. Green screen video effect is synonyms with _________ .
   (A) Morphing
   (B) Chroma key animation
   (C) Stop-motion animation
   (D) Cel-shading

2. The ratio of the _________ in an image is known as Aspect Ratio.
   (A) Horizontal points to product of 'horizontal and vertical' points
   (B) Horizontal to vertical points
   (C) Vertical to sum of 'horizontal and vertical' points
   (D) All of these

3. Stopping an animated character for a specific number of frames is called _________ .
   (A) Freezing
   (B) Slowing
   (C) Pacing
   (D) Panning

4. _________ is a graphics and image handling procedure, in which one image is gradually turned into another.
   (A) Animation
   (B) Morphing
   (C) Multimedia
   (D) Universal

5. In which of the following activities interactive media is applied?
   (A)
   (B)
   (C)
   (D) All of these

6. Software or hardware filters that adjust the loudness of specific audio frequencies are called _________.
   (A) Equalizers
   (B) Boosters
   (C) Acousters
   (D) Compound meters

7. In computer graphics, ZUI stands for _________ .
   (A) Zoomed Used Internet
   (B) Zoomable User Interface
   (C) Zoomable User Interaction
   (D) Zoomed User Interchange

8. _________ category of multimedia progresses without any navigational control.
   (A) Linear
   (B) Non-linear
   (C) Continuous
   (D) Non-continuous

9. In multimedia terminology, _________ is an invisible line, drawn along a character's pose, so that the character's pose will follow along the line.

(A) Keyframe
(B) Line of flow
(C) Line of action
(D) Layer

10. Which of the following statements is CORRECT?
(A) Random scan monitors draw a picture one line at a time.
(B) Raster scan monitors are known as vector displays.
(C) Raster scan monitors draw a picture one line at a time.
(D) Random scan is better suited for displaying shading and color areas.

11. What do you understand by the term breakdown?
(A) A type of animation technique in which a symmetry is defined in a character's pose.
(B) A very specific type of in-between that links two keyframes.
(C) The last step of animation, where sequence of all the layer is defined.
(D) The process of building a template of the character to be animated.

12. Repeating the same action to get a maximum screen time-out of a minimum of moves is called _________ .
(A) Cut-out animation
(B) Track animation
(C) Block animation
(D) Cycle animation

13. Playing movie through DVD that allows you to go forward and backward is an example of ______ media.
(A) Contiguous
(B) Non-contiguous
(C) Non-Linear
(D) Linear

14. The distinction between a graphic and a movie clip is that ________ .
(A) A graphic is static or stationary whereas a movie is dynamic
(B) Movie clip is static or stationary whereas a graphic is dynamic
(C) There is no difference between a graphic and a movie clip
(D) None of these

15. Motion graphics ________ .
(A) Refers to any moving / animated graphics created by use of digital sequencing of frames
(B) Is a term interchangeably used with animation
(C) Tends to encompass all animated movies
(D) All of these

Achievers Section (HOTS)

16. Which of the following statements best describes cutout animations?
(A) Cutouts are created from existing objects. Then these cutouts are automatically moved.
(B) Cutouts are stationary. A moving movie camera is focused on the cut-out and the animated scene is captured.
(C) Cutouts are arranged on flat surfaces. They are then moved and repositioned. This way animation is simulated.
(D) There exists no animation technique such as cutout animations.

17. The products and services on digital computer based system that uses technology like streaming media and responds to user actions by presenting content in the form of text, animation or images is called ___________.

(A) Monomedia (B) Footage
(C) Rich Media (D) Stagnant Media

18. It is one of the major problem faced by new animators, where they end up making the one half of an animated character's body to move and behave like its other half, making the character appearance unnatural. What is it called?
(A) Twinning (B) Morphing
(C) Scaling (D) Tuning

19. ________ is an anti-aliasing technique. It allows shift of 1/4, 1/2 and 3/4 of a pixel diameter. This enables a closer path of a line.
(A) Pixel phasing
(B) Filtering
(C) Intensity compensation
(D) Sampling technique

20. Identify the following:
– It is a technique to create an illusion of animation.
– In this a series of picture (gradually different from other) is drawn on every page of a book.
– All these pictures appear to animate when pages are turned rapidly.
(A) Motion Book (B) Roto Book
(C) Flip Book (D) Random Book

☺☺☺

Darken your choice with HB Pencil

1.	Ⓐ Ⓑ Ⓒ Ⓓ	7.	Ⓐ Ⓑ Ⓒ Ⓓ	13.	Ⓐ Ⓑ Ⓒ Ⓓ	19.	Ⓐ Ⓑ Ⓒ Ⓓ
2.	Ⓐ Ⓑ Ⓒ Ⓓ	8.	Ⓐ Ⓑ Ⓒ Ⓓ	14.	Ⓐ Ⓑ Ⓒ Ⓓ	20.	Ⓐ Ⓑ Ⓒ Ⓓ
3.	Ⓐ Ⓑ Ⓒ Ⓓ	9.	Ⓐ Ⓑ Ⓒ Ⓓ	15.	Ⓐ Ⓑ Ⓒ Ⓓ		
4.	Ⓐ Ⓑ Ⓒ Ⓓ	10.	Ⓐ Ⓑ Ⓒ Ⓓ	16.	Ⓐ Ⓑ Ⓒ Ⓓ		
5.	Ⓐ Ⓑ Ⓒ Ⓓ	11.	Ⓐ Ⓑ Ⓒ Ⓓ	17.	Ⓐ Ⓑ Ⓒ Ⓓ		
6.	Ⓐ Ⓑ Ⓒ Ⓓ	12.	Ⓐ Ⓑ Ⓒ Ⓓ	18.	Ⓐ Ⓑ Ⓒ Ⓓ		

CHAPTER

4

FLASH CS6

1. Which of the following statements is NOT true in case of Flash?
   (A) Flash files loads faster than animated GIF images.
   (B) It is a free software.
   (C) It allows interactivity compared to animated images.
   (D) It does not require significant programming skills.
2. Which of the following operations can be applied to layers?
   (A) You can change the position and order of layers.
   (B) You can delete layers.
   (C) You can add layers.
   (D) All of these
3. Which of the following operations performs the following tasks?
   (i) Generate the compressed version of your file with swf extension.
   (ii) Generate an HTML document that activates swf files and specifies browser settings.
   (A) Font Mapping (B) Publish
   (C) Snapping (D) Magnification
4. Which tool will you use in Flash CS6 to show "Inverse kinematics" effect?
   (A) (B)
   (C) (D)
5. You can scale, rotate and change the direction of the gradient fill in an object using the ________ tool.
   (A) Gradient Transform
   (B) Gradient Fill
   (C) Polystar
   (D) Free Transform
6. Which of the following is NOT a part of the Pen Tool flyout?
   (A) Add Anchor Point Tool
   (B) Delete Anchor Point Tool
   (C) Pin Anchor Point
   (D) Convert Anchor Point Tool
7. In ________ layers, you can create strokes that acts as a path for instances, groups or text to be followed.
   (A) Guide (B) Flip
   (C) Both (A) and (B) (D) None of these
8. To slow in and slow out the speed of an object in an animation, use ________ .
   (A) Flipping (B) Curving
   (C) Tweening (D) Easing
9. The default frame rate in Flash is ________ fps.
   (A) 18 (B) 24
   (C) 30 (D) 36
10. When you use geometrical primitives such as lines, curves, points and shapes to create graphics, you are using ________ graphics.

(A) Raster
(B) Linear
(C) Vector
(D) Collateral

11. Which of the following is NOT a filter type?
(A) Bevel
(B) Gradient Glow
(C) Gradient Shadow
(D) Gradient Bevel

12. To import elements on the stage, use the ________ key combination.

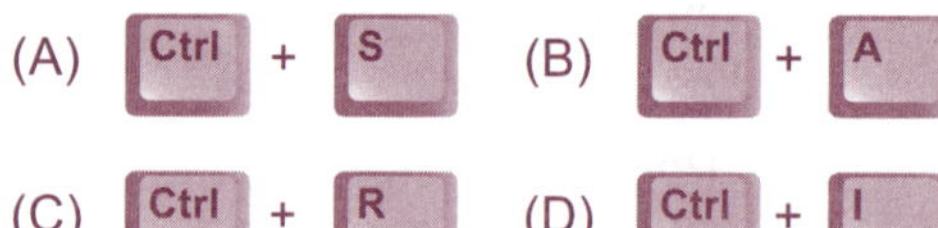

(A) Ctrl + S (B) Ctrl + A
(C) Ctrl + R (D) Ctrl + I

13. Match the following hot key sequences given in Column-I with the operations they perform in Column-II.

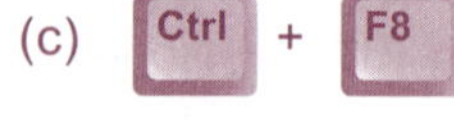

	Column - I	Column - II
(a)	Ctrl + B	(i) Group elements
(b)	Ctrl + G	(ii) Convert objects to symbols
(c)	Ctrl + F8	(iii) Create new symbols
(d)	F8	(iv) Break apart elements

(A) (a) – (iii), (b) – (i), (c) – (ii), (d) – (iv)
(B) (a) – (i), (b) – (iii), (c) – (ii), (d) – (iv)
(C) (a) – (ii), (b) – (i), (c) – (iii), (d) – (iv)
(D) (a) – (iv), (b) – (i), (c) – (iii), (d) – (ii)

14. Which of the following is also called as symbol store house?
(A) Timeline
(B) Library
(C) Stage
(D) Scene

15. The ________ symbol is used for animating static images.
(A) Static
(B) Instance
(C) Graphic
(D) Both (A) and (B)

Achievers Section (HOTS)

16. In which of the following area you found the set of options shown in given image?

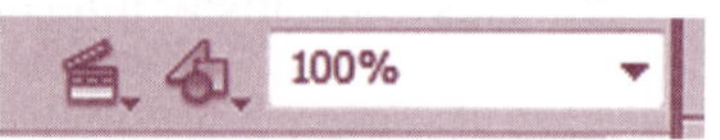

(A) Stage
(B) Timeline Window
(C) Motion Editor
(D) Tools Panel

17. You have created a shape on stage, now you want to add a filter effect to it. How would you do so?
(A) Convert the shape to Graphic symbol → Select the symbol → Go to Properties tab → Filter → Click on Add filter → Select the desired effect.
(B) Convert the shape to Movie Clip symbol → Select the symbol → Go to Properties → Filter → Click on Add filter → Select the desired effect
(C) Convert the shape to Graphic symbol → Select the symbol → Go to Modify tab → Filter → Click on Add filter → Select the desired effect.
(D) Convert the shape to Movie Clip symbol → Select the symbol → Go to Edit tab → Filter → Click on Add filter → Select the desired effect

18. To maintain a constant orientation of an object with respect to its path, use the ________ check box in the Properties window of Motion Tween.

(A) Scale (B) Snap
(C) Orient to path (D) Sync

19. What would happen when you select a line of text and then go to Modify tab and select "Break Apart" option?

(A) The text block will get broken into multiple text blocks to edit each character separately.

(B) The text block will get broken into two parts and each part will get assigned to a separate layer.

(C) The animation or any effect applied to the text will get removed.

(D) The text will get copied to all existing layers.

20. Select the CORRECT match.

(A) – Bind two objects together

(B) – Add a new object to a group

(C) – Add a shadow effect to a button

(D) – Used to add quick graphic patterns.

Darken your choice with HB Pencil

1.	Ⓐ Ⓑ Ⓒ Ⓓ	7.	Ⓐ Ⓑ Ⓒ Ⓓ	13.	Ⓐ Ⓑ Ⓒ Ⓓ	19.	Ⓐ Ⓑ Ⓒ Ⓓ
2.	Ⓐ Ⓑ Ⓒ Ⓓ	8.	Ⓐ Ⓑ Ⓒ Ⓓ	14.	Ⓐ Ⓑ Ⓒ Ⓓ	20.	Ⓐ Ⓑ Ⓒ Ⓓ
3.	Ⓐ Ⓑ Ⓒ Ⓓ	9.	Ⓐ Ⓑ Ⓒ Ⓓ	15.	Ⓐ Ⓑ Ⓒ Ⓓ		
4.	Ⓐ Ⓑ Ⓒ Ⓓ	10.	Ⓐ Ⓑ Ⓒ Ⓓ	16.	Ⓐ Ⓑ Ⓒ Ⓓ		
5.	Ⓐ Ⓑ Ⓒ Ⓓ	11.	Ⓐ Ⓑ Ⓒ Ⓓ	17.	Ⓐ Ⓑ Ⓒ Ⓓ		
6.	Ⓐ Ⓑ Ⓒ Ⓓ	12.	Ⓐ Ⓑ Ⓒ Ⓓ	18.	Ⓐ Ⓑ Ⓒ Ⓓ		

CHAPTER 5

INTRODUCTION TO VISUAL BASIC

1. What would be the value of variable res after execution?
   res = 9 Mod 2 + 1 – 2
   (A) –1 (B) 3
   (C) 0 (D) 4

2. A _______ is the primary work area where a user draws a GUI interface by placing several controls.
   (A) Toolbox
   (B) Form window
   (C) Project window
   (D) Properties

3. An environment that contains all tools and characteristics needed to create, run and test your program is called a/an ______ .
   (A) IDE (B) OOD
   (C) OOP (D) EIDE

4. What is the base of a user interface in a Visual Basic application?
   (A) Lable
   (B) Text Box
   (C) Command Button
   (D) Form

5. A VB application works in three modes. Which among the following is NOT a valid mode?
   (A) Design mode
   (B) Run mode
   (C) Interaction mode
   (D) Break/suspended mode

6. The statements which control the flow of execution of a program are called conditional statements. VB provides two conditional statements which are_____ .
   (A) If _ _ Then _ _ Else and Select Case
   (B) If _ _ Then _ _ Else and Do While
   (C) Select Case and For _ _ Next
   (D) For Next and Do _ _ Loop

7. In Visual Basic, the key to display the Properties window is _________ .
   (A) F2 (B) F4
   (C) F5 (D) F8

8. What is the output of the following Visual Basic code?
   ```
   Print Replace("Hello-World", 
      "-", "/")
   ```
   (A) HelloWorld (B) Hello/World
   (C) Hello World (D) helloworld

9. Observe the snapshot shown here and identify which of the marked areas when clicked will open the Form Layout window?

   Query Diagram Tools Add-Ins Window Help
   ① ② ③ ④

   (A) ① (B) ②
   (C) ③ (D) ④

10. Select the INCORRECT match.
   (A) Image tool - 
   (B) Label -
   (C) Text box -
   (D) Frame -

11. __________ is used to display some text.
   (A) Label (B) Toolbox
   (C) Properties (D) IDE

12. Which of the following lines of code will display an input box and then store the value entered in an Input Box into a variable *n* of integer type?
   (A) n = Input Box ("Enter number", Input, 0)
   (B) Input Box ('Enter number", Input, 0) = n
   (C) n = Val (Input Box ("Enter number", Input, 0))
   (D) All of these

13. Match the components given in Column-I with the functions they provide given in Column-II.

	Column-I		Column-II
(a)	Form window	(i)	To write the instructions for any object.
(b)	Properties window	(ii)	Displays a list of forms and other objects that constitute an application.
(c)	Project Explorer window	(iii)	Used to place various controls on a blank area
(d)	Code window	(iv)	Used to set the characteristics of forms and other controls placed on them.

   (A) (a) – (iv), (b) – (iii), (c) – (i), (d) – (ii)
   (B) (a) – (iv), (b) – (i), (c) – (ii), (d) – (iii)
   (C) (a) – (iii), (b) – (iv), (c) – (ii), (d) – (i)
   (D) (a) – (iv), (b) – (i), (c) – (iii), (d) – (ii)

14. Given here is the syntax of message box. What value should be entered for style value. If you want to display yes and no command buttons on the message box?
   MsgBox (Prompt, style value, title)
   (A) 0 (B) 1
   (C) 3 (D) 4

15. Which of the statements marked as Line 1, Line 2, Line 3 and Line 4 will cause an error?

```
Line 1    If A > 20
Line 2    A = A + 1
          Else
Line 3    A = A + 2
Line 4    Print A
          End If
```

   (A) Line 1 (B) Line 2
   (C) Line 3 (D) Line 4

Achievers Section (HOTS)

16. You have designed a form in VB and now you want to view where it will be positioned on the screen at run time. Which of the following is a tool available in VB that gives you a thumbnail view of the current form and also let you move this thumbnail to change the position of form?
   (A) Project Explorer
   (B) Menu Bar
   (C) Form Layout window
   (D) Object Browser

17. The form interface in Visual Basic is shown here that adds the two numbers entered by the user. Which of the following codes is correct for adding two numbers?

Assume the Name property of the controls as :

(a) First Number TextBox : Text1
(b) Second Number TextBox : Text2
(c) Answer TextBox : Text3
(d) add Command Button : cmdAdd

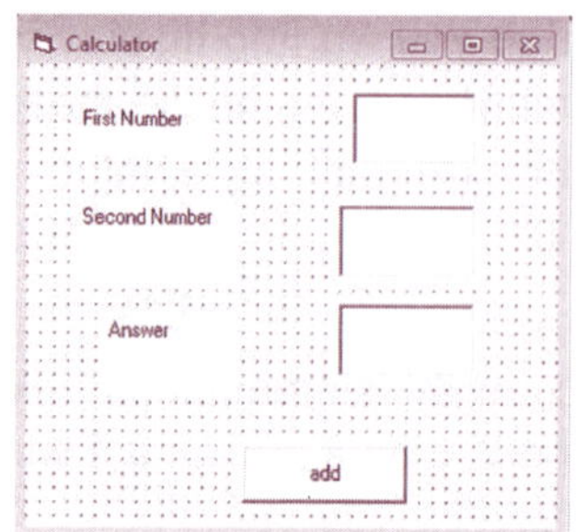

(A) Private Sub cmdAdd_Click()
Text3.Text=Val(Text1.Text)+Val(Text2.Text)
End Sub

(B) Private Sub cmdAdd_Click()
Text1.Text=Val(Text1.Text)+Val(Text3.Text)
End Sub

(C) Private Sub cmdAdd_Click()
Text1.Text=Val(Text2.Text), Add, Val(Text3.Text)
End Sub

(D) Both (B) and (C)

18. In Visual Basic, what value of the ScrollBars property in the properties of the textbox indicates that both horizontal and vertical scrollbars are included if you have set the MultiLine property as True?

(A) 0 (B) 1
(C) 2 (D) 3

19. Which of the following string functions returns the numbers contained in a string as numeric values?

(A) Val( ) (B) Instr( )
(C) Len( ) (D) Digit( )

20. Select the CORRECT match.

(A) Int() – Converts a number into integer by truncating its decimal part
(B) Round() – Rounds up an integer to a decimal number
(C) Instr() – Searches for string within a string and then replace it.
(D) Trim () – Remove space in between two words

Darken your choice with HB Pencil

1.	Ⓐ Ⓑ Ⓒ Ⓓ	7.	Ⓐ Ⓑ Ⓒ Ⓓ	13.	Ⓐ Ⓑ Ⓒ Ⓓ	19.	Ⓐ Ⓑ Ⓒ Ⓓ
2.	Ⓐ Ⓑ Ⓒ Ⓓ	8.	Ⓐ Ⓑ Ⓒ Ⓓ	14.	Ⓐ Ⓑ Ⓒ Ⓓ	20.	Ⓐ Ⓑ Ⓒ Ⓓ
3.	Ⓐ Ⓑ Ⓒ Ⓓ	9.	Ⓐ Ⓑ Ⓒ Ⓓ	15.	Ⓐ Ⓑ Ⓒ Ⓓ		
4.	Ⓐ Ⓑ Ⓒ Ⓓ	10.	Ⓐ Ⓑ Ⓒ Ⓓ	16.	Ⓐ Ⓑ Ⓒ Ⓓ		
5.	Ⓐ Ⓑ Ⓒ Ⓓ	11.	Ⓐ Ⓑ Ⓒ Ⓓ	17.	Ⓐ Ⓑ Ⓒ Ⓓ		
6.	Ⓐ Ⓑ Ⓒ Ⓓ	12.	Ⓐ Ⓑ Ⓒ Ⓓ	18.	Ⓐ Ⓑ Ⓒ Ⓓ		

CHAPTER

6 HTML

1. Consider the statement given here.

<a href = "http://www.yahoo.com/">Link</a>

① ② ③ ④

Which of the parts marked by numbers ①, ②, ③ and ④ would get displayed in the webpage?

(A) ① (B) ②

(C) ③ (D) ④

2. What would be the output of the given HTML code?

```
<HTML>
<hr size=4 color=black width=50%>
<h1 align=center> COMPUTER WORLD
</h1>
<hr size=4 color=black width=50%>
</HTML>
```

(A) **COMPUTER WORLD**

(B) **COMPUTER WORLD**

(C) **COMPUTER WORLD**

(D) **COMPUTER WORLD**

3. If you use ____________, by default the items will be displayed in bulleted form.

(A) <bl> and </bl>

(B) <b> and </b>

(C) <li> and </li>

(D) <th> and </th>

4. To convert the text 'Science Olympiad Foundation', to a hyperlink to www.sofworld.org, use __________ .

(A) <a>http://www.sofworld.org</a>

(B) <a href="http://www.sofworld.org">Science Olympiad Foundation</a>

(C) <a name="http://www.sofworld.org">sofworld.org</a>

(D) <a url="http://www.sofworld.org">Science Olympiad Foundation</a>

5. The img tag is used for displaying an image in a webpage. The CORRECT use of the img tag is _________ .

(A) <img src="imagename.format" alt=" This is an image" height = "45" width = "45">

(B) </img src="imageurl.html">< alt="This is an image", height = "45", width = "45"/>

(C) <image src=imagename.gif,alt="This is an image"> <height = "45">, <width = "45"/>

(D) <img ="imagename.format" height = "45", width = "45">

6. Select the INCORRECT match.

(A) <href> – Defines the link address

(B) <target> – Defines where to open the link document

(C) <a> – Defines the link

(D) <alt> – Defines the alternate link address

7. The statement <Body text = Blue> will set the ________ .
   (A) Text color to blue
   (B) Color of title text to blue
   (C) Background color to blue
   (D) Link color to blue

8. What does the following line of an HTML code will do?

   <body vlink =red>

   (A) Sets the visited link color to red
   (B) Sets the displayed link color to red
   (C) Sets the active link color to red
   (D) None of these

9. Which of the following is the CORRECT statement?
   (A) <a href= "mypage.html">mypage </a>
   (B) <a href= "mypage.html" target= "_ blank"> mypage </a>
   (C) <a href= "mypage.html"> alt = "mypage" mypage</a>
   (D) Both (A) and (B)

10. To add cells in a row of a table use ________ tag.
   (A) <cell> (B) <col>
   (C) <td> (D) <val>

11. You can use the ________ tags to add rows to your tables.
   (A) <td> and </td> (B) <cr> and </cr>
   (C) <th> and </th> (D) <tr> and </tr>

12. Which of the following is/are attributes of <a> tag?
   (A) href (B) name
   (C) src (D) Both (A) and (B)

13. Which of the following tags can be used inside a <td> tag?
   (A) <p> (B) <ul>
   (C) <ol> (D) All of these

14. An html table may include ________ element/elements.
   (A) <caption> (B) <thead>
   (C) <tbody> (D) All of these

15. The space between a cell's border and its contents can be controlled when the ________ attribute is used.
   (A) Cellspacing (B) Cellpadding
   (C) Colspan (D) Rowspan

Achievers Section (HOTS)

16. Which of the following is NOT a valid value of frame attribute of <table> tag?
   (A) void (B) hsides
   (C) box (D) around

17. The statement given below creates a name to a section "NCO". Which of the following is the CORRECT code, if you want to link the given named section in HTML?

   <A name="NCO">NCO</A>

   (A) <A href="#NCO">Link to NCO</A>
   (B) <href="#NCO">Link to NCO
   (C) <A href=NCO>Link to NCO</A>
   (D) <A href="NCO">Link to NCO</A>

18. ______ attribute of <table> tag is used to specify the background color of a table.
   (A) rel (B) bgcolor
   (C) tbgcolor (D) tablebg

19. What will be the output of the given HTML code?

```
<HTML>
<BODY>
<TABLE BORDER = "1">
<CAPTION><BIG>Employee Record
</BIG></CAPTION>
<TR>
<TH>Name</TH>
<TH>Age</TH>
</TR>
<TR>
<TD>Ashish</TD>
<TD>18</TD>
```

```
</TR>
</TABLE>
</BODY>
</HTML>
```

(A) Employee Record

Name	Age
Ashish	18

(B) **Employee Record**

Name	**Age**
Ashish	18

(C) **Employee Record**

Name	Age
Ashish	18

(D) *Employee Record*

Name	**Age**
Ashish	18

20. What would be the output of the given HTML code?

```
<table frame="vsides">
<tr><th>National Cyber Olympiad</th></tr>
</table>
```

(A) | **National Cyber Olympiad** |

(B) **National Cyber Olympiad** (underlined)

(C) **National Cyber Olympiad** (double underlined)

(D) **National Cyber Olympiad** |

☺☺☺

Darken your choice with HB Pencil

1.	Ⓐ Ⓑ Ⓒ Ⓓ	7.	Ⓐ Ⓑ Ⓒ Ⓓ	13.	Ⓐ Ⓑ Ⓒ Ⓓ	19.	Ⓐ Ⓑ Ⓒ Ⓓ
2.	Ⓐ Ⓑ Ⓒ Ⓓ	8.	Ⓐ Ⓑ Ⓒ Ⓓ	14.	Ⓐ Ⓑ Ⓒ Ⓓ	20.	Ⓐ Ⓑ Ⓒ Ⓓ
3.	Ⓐ Ⓑ Ⓒ Ⓓ	9.	Ⓐ Ⓑ Ⓒ Ⓓ	15.	Ⓐ Ⓑ Ⓒ Ⓓ		
4.	Ⓐ Ⓑ Ⓒ Ⓓ	10.	Ⓐ Ⓑ Ⓒ Ⓓ	16.	Ⓐ Ⓑ Ⓒ Ⓓ		
5.	Ⓐ Ⓑ Ⓒ Ⓓ	11.	Ⓐ Ⓑ Ⓒ Ⓓ	17.	Ⓐ Ⓑ Ⓒ Ⓓ		
6.	Ⓐ Ⓑ Ⓒ Ⓓ	12.	Ⓐ Ⓑ Ⓒ Ⓓ	18.	Ⓐ Ⓑ Ⓒ Ⓓ		

CHAPTER 7

MS-WORD 2010

1. How to edit text in Full Screen Reading view?
   (A) By default, editing is permitted in full screen mode, so we do not have to make any changes.
   (B) After selecting Full Screen Reading view, click on View Options and select

   (C) After selecting Full Screen Reading view, click on View Options and select

   (D) After selecting Full Screen Reading view, click on View Options and select

2. For which of the following purpose the given icon is used?

   AB¹

   (A) To assign hyperlinks in a document that are created to perform repetitive tasks.
   (B) To add a numbered node at the end of a page, which gets automatically renumbered as the text move around the document.
   (C) To add a line of text below or above a graphical object.
   (D) To increase the number of comments that were inserted in a document.

3. When you press Alt + Ctrl + D keys in a document then _________ .
   (A) An endnote reference mark will get inserted in the document.
   (B) A footnote reference mark will get inserted in the document
   (C) Draft view will get enabled
   (D) The document will get split in two parts

4. Which of the following steps will allow you to combine multiple versions of a document?
   (A) Review tab → Compare group → click on drop-down arrow of 'Compare' → click on 'Combine'
   (B) Review tab → Changes group → click on drop-down arrow of 'Changes' → click on 'Combine'
   (C) Review tab → Changes group → click on 'Merge'
   (D) Review tab → Changes group → click on drop-down arrow of 'Combine' → select versions of document → click on 'Combine'

5. Which of the following is the CORRECT way to open 'Restrict Formatting and Editing' pane?
   (A) References tab → Protect group → click on 'Restrict Editing'

(B) Review tab → Protect group → click on 'Restrict Editing'
(C) Review tab → Restrict group → click on 'Restrict Editing'
(D) Both (A) and (C)

6. Pressing Ctrl + Shift + E keys will ________.
(A) Turn on or off the Reviewing Pane
(B) Open the Word Count dialog box
(C) Open the Styles Task pane
(D) Turn on or off the Track Changes feature

7. Priyanka wants to match the width of the document with the width of the window. Which of the following options available in View tab will allow her to do so?
(A) Arrange Width (B) Match Width
(C) Zoom Page (D) Page Width

8. Using _____ you can search through your document.
(A) Navigation Pane
(B) Searching Pane
(C) Find Pane
(D) Document Pane

9. What would happen when you perform the following steps in a document?
Go to Review tab → Tracking Group → Show Markup → Uncheck "Formatting" option
(A) It will disable the formatting option available on the ribbon.
(B) It will remove all the formatting applied to the document leaving only the plain text.
(C) It will hide formatting changes which were made to the document when Track Changes option was enabled.
(D) Both (A) and (B)

10. Which of the following MS-Word features will save information in every few minutes so that you do not lose data?
(A) AutoPreserve
(B) AutoPrevent Save
(C) AutoRecover
(D) AutoSave

11. Which of the following options breaks lines between the syllables of words to have more uniform spacing between the words in MS-Word 2010?
(A) 
(B) 
(C) 
(D) 

12. The icon marked as 'A' in the given image of Reviewing Pane can be used to _____.

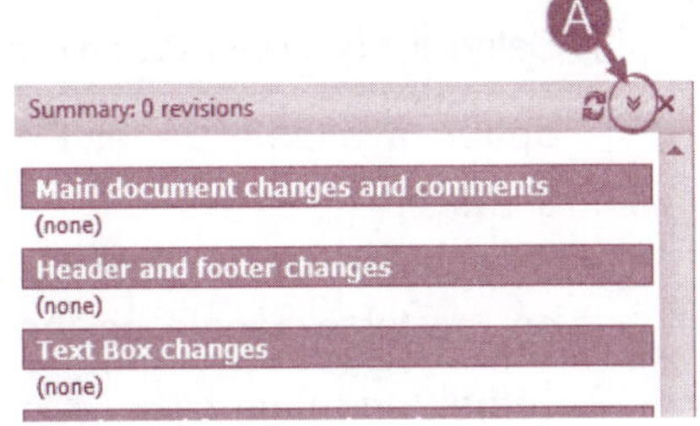

(A) Show/hide detailed summary of each type of changes made to the document
(B) Show/hide the Reviewing Pane
(C) Refresh all the changes made to the document
(D) Move the Reviewing Pane

13. Which Pagination options forces a paragraph to appear with the paragraph that follows it in MS-Word 2010?
(A) Keep lines together
(B) Widow/Orphan control
(C) Keep with next
(D) Page break before

14. Which of the following properties can be checked using Inspect document feature available in File tab?
    (i) Revision marks such as comments
    (ii) Author name
    (iii) Header, footer or watermarks
    (A) Only (i) (B) Only (ii)
    (C) Only (iii)
    (D) All (i),(ii) and (iii)

15. To horizontally center the table on a page ___________ .
    (A) Select first cell and click [icon] option available under Paragraph group of Table tab
    (B) Select the first row and click [icon] option available under Paragraph group of Home tab
    (C) Select the first column and click [icon] option available under Paragraph group of Home tab
    (D) Select the whole table by clicking on the table handle on the top left corner, and then click [icon] option available under Paragraph group of Home tab

Achievers Section (HOTS)

16. Swati is making a document in MS-Word 2010 and now she wants to insert an image, in such a way that whatever changes she makes to source file of image, shall reflect in Word also. However, she does not want that if the original file is deleted, the image from Word document also gets deleted. Which of the following options she should select to achieve this?
    (A) Insert tab → Illustrations group → Picture → click on Insert dropdown arrow → Insert.
    (B) Insert tab → Illustrations group → Picture → click on Insert dropdown arrow → Link to File.
    (C) Insert tab → Illustrations group → Picture → click on Insert dropdown arrow → Insert and Link.
    (D) Insert tab → Illustrations group → Picture → click on Insert dropdown arrow → Image.

17. While tracking changes, to view all the changes in header and footer area of a document use ________.
    (A) Research Pane
    (B) Reviewing Pane
    (C) Show Markup
    (D) Changes Pane

18. You want to share a copy of a Word document with one of your friend, who has an older version of MS-Word. Which of the following options present in Word Options will let you embed the font to maintain the look of document in earlier version?
    (A) Preseve Fidelity
    (B) Auto correct options
    (C) Page display option
    (D) Start up option

19. Match the following.

	Column - I		Column - II
(a)	π	(i)	Make text look like as it is marked with a highlighter pen.
(b)	Ω	(ii)	Change the set of styles, colors and fonts used in the document.

(c) 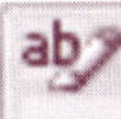 (iii) Insert symbols that are not on your keyboard, such as copyright symbols, trademark symbols, paragraph marks, and unicode characters.

(d)   (iv) Select text or objects in the document.

(e) 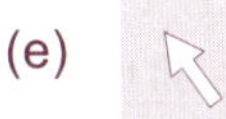 (v) Insert common mathematical equations or build up your own equations using a library of math symbols.

(A) (a) – (v), (b) – (iii), (c) – (i), (d) – (ii), (e) – (iv)

(B) (a) – (v), (b) – (iii), (c) – (iv), (d) – (i), (e) – (ii)

(C) (a) – (iii), (b) – (v), (c) – (iv), (d) – (ii), (e) – (i)

(D) (a) – (iii), (b) – (v), (c) – (i), (d) – (ii), (e) – (iv)

20. Which of the following statements hold(s) true about the portion marked as P in the given snapshot?

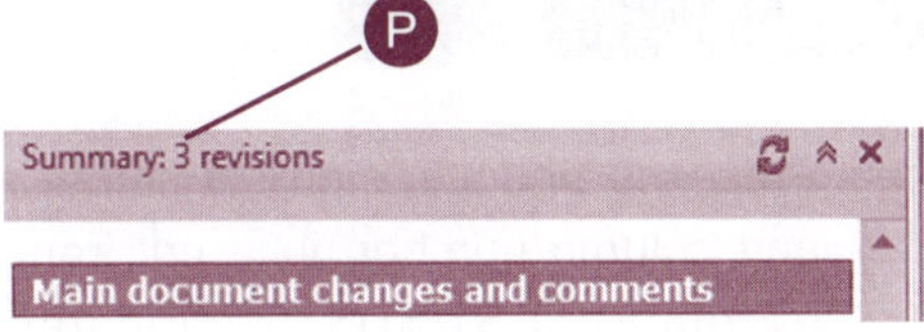

Statement 1 : It displays the total number of changes in the form of insertion, deletion, header footer changes, etc.

Statement 2 : It indicates that a document can be edit only three times.

(A) Only Statement 1

(B) Only Statement 2

(C) Both Statement 1 and Statement 2

(D) Neither Statement 1 nor Statement 2

Darken your choice with HB Pencil

1.	Ⓐ Ⓑ Ⓒ Ⓓ	**7.**	Ⓐ Ⓑ Ⓒ Ⓓ	**13.**	Ⓐ Ⓑ Ⓒ Ⓓ	**19.**	Ⓐ Ⓑ Ⓒ Ⓓ
2.	Ⓐ Ⓑ Ⓒ Ⓓ	**8.**	Ⓐ Ⓑ Ⓒ Ⓓ	**14.**	Ⓐ Ⓑ Ⓒ Ⓓ	**20.**	Ⓐ Ⓑ Ⓒ Ⓓ
3.	Ⓐ Ⓑ Ⓒ Ⓓ	**9.**	Ⓐ Ⓑ Ⓒ Ⓓ	**15.**	Ⓐ Ⓑ Ⓒ Ⓓ		
4.	Ⓐ Ⓑ Ⓒ Ⓓ	**10.**	Ⓐ Ⓑ Ⓒ Ⓓ	**16.**	Ⓐ Ⓑ Ⓒ Ⓓ		
5.	Ⓐ Ⓑ Ⓒ Ⓓ	**11.**	Ⓐ Ⓑ Ⓒ Ⓓ	**17.**	Ⓐ Ⓑ Ⓒ Ⓓ		
6.	Ⓐ Ⓑ Ⓒ Ⓓ	**12.**	Ⓐ Ⓑ Ⓒ Ⓓ	**18.**	Ⓐ Ⓑ Ⓒ Ⓓ		

CHAPTER 8

MS-EXCEL 2010

1. Presence of dollar sign ($) before a row and column number, in a cell range for example, $C$7:$D$10 indicates that ________.
   (A) An absolute cell reference is created
   (B) Cell address will change when it is copied to another cell
   (C) The sheet tab is changed
   (D) The status bar does not display the cell address

2. Which of the following options will allow you to force the user to choose the value of a selected cell from the specified drop-down list in MS-Excel 2010?
   (A) Data Validation
   (B) Consolidate
   (C) What-If Analysis
   (D) Subtotal

3. To do What-If-Analysis, which of the following Data Tools can you use?
   (A) Data Table
   (B) Goal Seek
   (C) Scenario Manager
   (D) All of these

4. What is Watch Window?
   (A) A separate window that remains visible to monitor the values of certain cells.
   (B) A resizable window that displays a list of all formulas used in a sheet.
   (C) A separate workbook that gets displayed when certain conditions are met.
   (D) A window that displays all the formula errors.

5. Identify the given icon.

   (A) Trace Dependents
   (B) Trace Precedents
   (C) Show Formulas
   (D) Calculate Result

6. ________ option allows you to view multiple distant parts of your worksheet at once.
   (A) Zoom to Selection
   (B) Page Layout View
   (C) Split
   (D) Zoom In

7. Which of the following options would replace the "?" to open the Watch Window?

   Formulas tab → ? → Watch Window

   (A) Calculations (B) Function
   (C) Formula Auditing (D) Data Tools

8. Which of the following options allows you to debug a formula by executing each part of the formula individually?
   (A) Evaluate Formula
   (B) Examine Formula
   (C) Auditing Formula
   (D) Checking Formula

9. Which of the following statements hold(s) true about 'Protect Sheet' feature?

Statement 1 : It can be used to protect the entire workbook by providing password.

Statement 2 : It can be used to protect the worksheet from unwanted changes.

(A) Only Statement 1
(B) Only Statement 2
(C) Both Statement 1 and Statement 2
(D) Neither Statement 1 nor Statement 2

10. is used to _________ .

(A) Insert a signature line to specify the person who must sign
(B) View the document in the full screen mode
(C) Edit the layout of the document
(D) Save a set of display and print settings

11. Which of the following statements is INCORRECT about 'Share Workbook' feature?

(A) It allows multiple people to work in a workbook at the same time.
(B) It requires workbook to be saved to a network location.
(C) Workbook that contains tables can be shared.
(D) Both (A) and (B)

12. What is the use of COUNTA function in MS-Excel 2010?

(A) It returns the number of blank cells in a range.
(B) It returns the number of blank cells on the entire worksheet.
(C) It returns the number of non-blank cells in a range.
(D) It returns the correlation between two data.

13. Match the following.

	Column - I		Column - II
(a)	Ctrl + Shift + & 7	(i)	Unhide hidden rows within the selection.
(b)	Ctrl + Shift + _ –	(ii)	Applies the outline border to selected cells.
(c)	Ctrl + Shift + ^ 6	(iii)	Removes the outline border from the selected cells.
(d)	Ctrl + Shift + (9	(iv)	Applies the exponential number format with two decimal places.

(A) (a) – (iv), (b) – (iii), (c) – (ii), (d) – (i)
(B) (a) – (ii), (b) – (iii), (c) – (iv), (d) – (i)
(C) (a) – (ii), (b) – (iii), (c) – (i), (d) – (iv)
(D) (a) – (ii), (b) – (i), (c) – (iv), (d) – (iii)

14. Which of the following statements hold(s) true about the given icon ?

Statement 1 : It is used to total several rows of related data together.

Statement 2 : The name of shown command button is sumdata.

(A) Only Statement 1
(B) Only Statement 2
(C) Both Statement 1 and Statement 2
(D) Neither Statement 1 nor Statement 2

15. What is the use of icon?

(A) It is used to trace errors
(B) It is used to remove arrows drawn by Trace Precedents

(C) It is used to remove arrows drawn by Trace Dependents

(D) Both (B) and (C)

Achievers Section (HOTS)

16. Reema wants to display formulas in cells instead of the resulting value. Which of the following steps will help her to do so?
    (A) Formulas tab → Formula Auditing group → click on
    (B) File tab → Options → Advanced → select 'Show formulas in cells instead of their calculated results' checkbox under 'Display options for this worksheet' section → OK
    (C) View tab → Display group → select 'Show Formulas' check box
    (D) Both (A) and (B)

17. Which MS-Excel tool will you use to combine values from multiple ranges into one new range?
    (A) (B)
    (C) (D)

18. Which of the following key combinations is used to ungroup a range of cells?

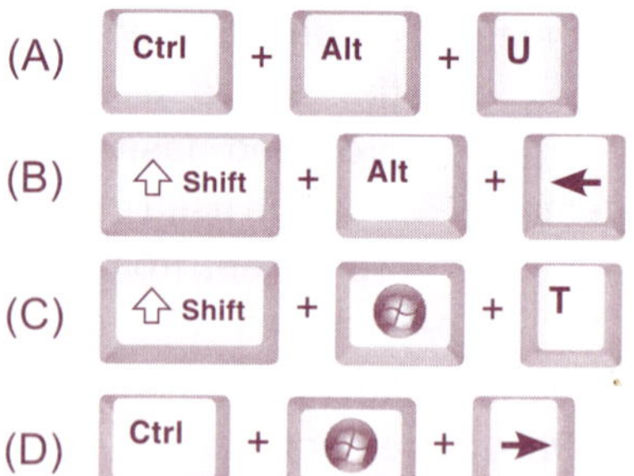

19. Rishab wants to add a condition to selected range of cells, such that when a user enters a value less than 0, it should display a message stating that only positive numbers can be entered. Which of the following can be used for this purpose?
    (A) Consolidate (B) Data Validation
    (C) Data Restriction (D) What-If Analysis

20. An organisation sells its products in three regions and the quarterly sales from each region is stored in three identical worksheets. Now, the sales team want to know the total sales of each product by adding sales from all regions. Which MS-Excel tool should be used for this purpose?
    (A) Goal Seek (B) Consolidate
    (C) Watch Window (D) Subtotal

☺☺☺

Darken your choice with HB Pencil

1.	Ⓐ Ⓑ Ⓒ Ⓓ	7.	Ⓐ Ⓑ Ⓒ Ⓓ	13.	Ⓐ Ⓑ Ⓒ Ⓓ	19.	Ⓐ Ⓑ Ⓒ Ⓓ
2.	Ⓐ Ⓑ Ⓒ Ⓓ	8.	Ⓐ Ⓑ Ⓒ Ⓓ	14.	Ⓐ Ⓑ Ⓒ Ⓓ	20.	Ⓐ Ⓑ Ⓒ Ⓓ
3.	Ⓐ Ⓑ Ⓒ Ⓓ	9.	Ⓐ Ⓑ Ⓒ Ⓓ	15.	Ⓐ Ⓑ Ⓒ Ⓓ		
4.	Ⓐ Ⓑ Ⓒ Ⓓ	10.	Ⓐ Ⓑ Ⓒ Ⓓ	16.	Ⓐ Ⓑ Ⓒ Ⓓ		
5.	Ⓐ Ⓑ Ⓒ Ⓓ	11.	Ⓐ Ⓑ Ⓒ Ⓓ	17.	Ⓐ Ⓑ Ⓒ Ⓓ		
6.	Ⓐ Ⓑ Ⓒ Ⓓ	12.	Ⓐ Ⓑ Ⓒ Ⓓ	18.	Ⓐ Ⓑ Ⓒ Ⓓ		

CHAPTER 9

MS-POWERPOINT 2010

1. To move a section in Slides Pane ____ .
   (A) Right click on the section name, then click Move Section Up or Move Section Down
   (B) Left click on the section name and drag it up or down to move it accordingly
   (C) Left click on the section name and press the up or down arrow key.
   (D) Both (A) and (B)

2. Which of the following options would you choose to achieve following tasks?
   (i) Display a laser pointer in Blue Color
   (ii) Advance slides using timings
   (iii) Set the slides to be shown during the slide show

   (A) 
   (B) 
   (C) 
   (D) 

3. If you have two copies of your presentation with some changes in both, you can combine the copy with your original presentation, and then accept or discard changes into the presentation. Which of the following features of PowerPoint will allow you to do this?
   (A) Track Changes
   (B) Document Inspector
   (C) Compare
   (D) Custom Animation

4. Which of the following is NOT a way to copy slides from other presentations in MS-PowerPoint 2010?
   (A) Open two PowerPoint windows side by side and drag and drop slides between them.
   (B) Open two PowerPoint windows, copy slides from one of them to the clipboard and then paste them into the other presentation.
   (C) Use the Duplicate Slide feature.
   (D) Use the Reuse Slides feature.

5. You can set the animation to start after you click a shape or when media playback reaches a bookmark. You can achieve this task by using ________ .

   (A) 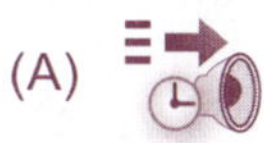
   (B) 
   (C) 
   (D) 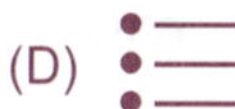

6. Which of the following steps is CORRECT to package a presentation for CD?
   (A) File → Save & Pack → File Types → Package Presentation for CD
   (B) File → Save & Pack → File Types → Publish Slides

(C) File → Save & Send → File Types → Package Presentation for CD
(D) File → Save & Go → File Types → Package Presentation for CD

7. In MS-PowerPoint 2010, while typing in a placeholder ______ option button automatically decreases the size of the font to fit it in the placeholder.
(A) Text (B) Auto Adjust
(C) AutoFill
(D) AutoFit Text to Placeholder

8. What is the main functional difference between the Notes Master and Handout Master views?
(A) You cannot move or resize slide placeholders on the Handout Master, whereas in Notes Master you can.
(B) In the Notes Master, you cannot format the slide placeholders, whereas in Handout Master you can.
(C) You cannot format Header placeholder in the Handout Master, whereas in Notes Master you can.
(D) You cannot change the slide orientation in the Handout Master, whereas in Handout Master you can.

9. Which of the following options available under 'Format' tab of 'Drawing Tools' is used to specify the color, width and line style for the outline of the text in text placeholders?
(A) (B) 
(C) (D) 

10. option available under 'Design' tab of 'SmartArt' Tools is used to ______.
(A) Convert Text to Flowchart
(B) Discard all the formatting changes made to SmartArt graphic
(C) Convert Shapes to Text
(D) Save all formatting changes

11. Which of the following action buttons can be added in a slide?
(i) (ii)
(iii)
(A) Only (i) (B) Only (ii)
(C) Only (iii)
(D) All (i), (ii) and (iii)

12. Select the INCORRECT match.
(A) - Adds comment about the selection
(B) - Ends the presentation review
(C) - Edit Comment
(D) - Checks the spelling of the text

13. What is legend in a chart?
(A) A formatting feature for chart title.
(B) A little box next to chart that describes what the different colors or patterns mean.
(C) Text that defines the category or the unit of measurement on an axis.
(D) Text that typically appears above the chart.

14. Which of the following options available in Timings group of Transitions tab is used to specify length of a transition?
(A) Release (B) Record
(C) Duration (D) Delay

15. Which of the following statements hold(s) true about the given icon?

Statement 1 : It is used for disabling all the transitions applied in a presentation.

Statement 2 : It is used for adding an action to an object.

(A) Only Statement 1
(B) Only Statement 2
(C) Both Statement 1 and Statement 2
(D) Neither Statement 1 nor Statement 2

Achievers Section (HOTS)

16. In MS-PowerPoint 2010, when the insertion point is flashing in a textbox, what should be pressed to select the text box itself?

(A) Alt (B) Esc
(C) Ctrl (D) Alt + Ctrl

17. Which of the following options of 'Save & Send' category of backstage view will allow you to store slides in a shared location, locate the latest version of slide, etc. in MS-PowerPoint 2010?

(A) (B)
(C) (D)

18. Megha is comparing two presentations using Compare feature. Now she wants to end the comparison by applying current accept and reject decisions. Which of the following options should be used for this purpose?

(A) End Review (B) End Compare
(C) Close Review (D) End

19. Geetika has inserted an image in a slide and she wants to convert the image into a SmartArt graphic. Which of the following options will help her to do so in MS-PowerPoint 2010?

(A) Picture Layout (B) Picture Effects
(C) Corrections (D) Artistic Effects

20. You can switch between Slides and Outline pane in Normal View by pressing ___ keys.

(A) Shift + Tab
(B) Ctrl + Tab
(C) Ctrl + Shift + Tab
(D) Shift + F4

☺☺☺

Darken your choice with HB Pencil

1.	Ⓐ Ⓑ Ⓒ Ⓓ	7.	Ⓐ Ⓑ Ⓒ Ⓓ	13.	Ⓐ Ⓑ Ⓒ Ⓓ	19.	Ⓐ Ⓑ Ⓒ Ⓓ
2.	Ⓐ Ⓑ Ⓒ Ⓓ	8.	Ⓐ Ⓑ Ⓒ Ⓓ	14.	Ⓐ Ⓑ Ⓒ Ⓓ	20.	Ⓐ Ⓑ Ⓒ Ⓓ
3.	Ⓐ Ⓑ Ⓒ Ⓓ	9.	Ⓐ Ⓑ Ⓒ Ⓓ	15.	Ⓐ Ⓑ Ⓒ Ⓓ		
4.	Ⓐ Ⓑ Ⓒ Ⓓ	10.	Ⓐ Ⓑ Ⓒ Ⓓ	16.	Ⓐ Ⓑ Ⓒ Ⓓ		
5.	Ⓐ Ⓑ Ⓒ Ⓓ	11.	Ⓐ Ⓑ Ⓒ Ⓓ	17.	Ⓐ Ⓑ Ⓒ Ⓓ		
6.	Ⓐ Ⓑ Ⓒ Ⓓ	12.	Ⓐ Ⓑ Ⓒ Ⓓ	18.	Ⓐ Ⓑ Ⓒ Ⓓ		

CHAPTER 10

INTERNET AND VIRUSES

1. What are the two important categories of resident virus?
   (A) Fast infectors, slow infectors
   (B) Macro infectors, micro infectors
   (C) Primary infectors, secondary infectors
   (D) File infectors, drive infectors

2. Which of the following software not only interrupts the normal working of a computer but also steals important data from it?
   (A) Antivirus software
   (B) Operating system
   (C) Antiware
   (D) Malware

3. Which of the following technologies uses encryption to protect the privacy of all your data transmissions between two points?
   (A) Secure Socket Layer
   (B) Virtual Private Network
   (C) Transport Layer Security
   (D) All of these

4. When you copy the address book contents of one of your mobile phones to another mobile phone, where both your phones are in your two hands, you may be using _______ technology.
   (A) Parallel (B) Bluetooth
   (C) Fidelity (D) Personal

5. Identify the virus.
   - It was distributed by David L. Smith.
   - It was distributed as e-mail attachment.

   (A) Melissa (B) Code Red
   (C) Blue Whale (D) ILOVEYOU

6. Rerouting from a requested site to an undesired site without your intervention is called _________ .
   (A) Pharming
   (B) Spamming
   (C) Hijacking
   (D) Trapping

7. A low power WLAN technology that facilitates interoperability among smartphones and portable consumer devices such as headphones fitness accessories and heart rate monitor. It is also called "Bluetooth 4.0".
   (A) Bluetooth Smart Ready
   (B) Bluetooth Berrycasting
   (C) Bluetooth Handoff
   (D) Podcasts

8. The technology that creates a secure and private connection between two or more computers is called a _________ .
   (A) Network Tethering
   (B) Encryption
   (C) FTP
   (D) Secure Socket Layer

9. _________ is a software used by attackers to gain administrative rights to a computer.
   (A) Root Kit (B) BIOS
   (C) Firmware (D) Adware

10. Identify the following:
   - It makes changes in a disk's file system.
   - It creates the illusion that virus has infected every program on the disk.
   - When a program is run from infected disk, it causes the virus to run as well.

   (A) Cluster Virus (B) Trojan horse
   (C) Melissa (D) Morris Worm

11. It was a computer worm whose primary's target were Internet server and it allowed attackers to have the same access to an infected machine as the current user. It was launched one week after 9/11 attack. Identify it.
   (A) Melissa (B) Code Red
   (C) Nimda (D) Sapphire

12. To access the internet, the ______ connects your computer to your phone line and provide access to the network.
   (A) Operating system
   (B) Browser
   (C) Modem (D) Repeater

13. Websites that allows you to edit / modify / create / delete content are called _________ .
   (A) Homepages (B) Digicast
   (C) Podcasts (D) Blogs

14. A collection of websites connected with hyperlinks and that forms the part of the internet is referred as ________ .
   (A) Browser (B) WWW
   (C) DNS (D) URL

15. Deliberately modifying the return address on an e-mail such that it seems to be coming from anyone but not the actual sender is called _________ .
   (A) Spoofing (B) Pharming
   (C) Spamming (D) Rootkit

Achievers Section (HOTS)

16. Match the following.

	Column - I		Column - II
(a)	Password	(i)	Detects and removes viruses and other malicious software from the computer.
(b)	Antivirus software	(ii)	Protects information by converting it into unreadable code that cannot be deciphered easily by unauthorized people.
(c)	Firewall	(iii)	Secret sequence of characters that enables a user to control access to a computer, program or file.
(d)	Disk Encryption	(iv)	A security system designed to protect a computer from hacker attacks.

   (A) (a) – (iv), (b) – (i), (c) – (iii), (d) – (ii)
   (B) (a) – (iv), (b) – (i), (c) – (ii), (d) – (iii)
   (C) (a) – (iv), (b) – (iii), (c) – (i), (d) – (ii)
   (D) (a) – (iii), (b) – (i), (c) – (iv), (d) – (ii)

17. In which of the following ways computer worm spreads?
   (i) Via e-mail attachments
   (ii) Via hyperlinks to web or any such source or network
   (iii) Via peer to peer networks

   (A) Only (i)
   (B) Only (ii)
   (C) Only (iii)
   (D) All (i), (ii) and (iii)

18. False reports about non-existent viruses, which claims how harmful the effect would be if suggested steps mentioned in the e-mails are not taken are called _______ .
(A) Hoax (B) Browser Object
(C) Cookies (D) Exploitholic

19. Match the following.

	Column - I		Column - II
(a)	Username	(i)	Worldwide system of servers
(b)	Hostname	(ii)	username@hostname
(c)	E-mail	(iii)	Unwanted e-mails
(d)	DNS	(iv)	Name given to the user
(e)	Spam	(v)	Name of the server

(A) (a) – (iv), (b) – (v), (c) – (ii), (d) – (i), (e) – (iii)
(B) (a) – (iv), (b) – (v), (c) – (iii), (d) – (i), (e) – (ii)
(C) (a) – (v), (b) – (iv), (c) – (iii), (d) – (ii), (e) – (i)
(D) (a) – (iv), (b) – (v), (c) – (iii), (d) – (ii), (e) – (i)

20. An antivirus is an important program for the safety of your computer, because it _______ .
(A) Prevents, defects and removes destructive programs
(B) Allocate, spread and create malware
(C) Wipes your data from hard disk
(D) Maintain the CMOS setting

☺☺☺

Darken your choice with HB Pencil

1.	Ⓐ Ⓑ Ⓒ Ⓓ	7.	Ⓐ Ⓑ Ⓒ Ⓓ	13.	Ⓐ Ⓑ Ⓒ Ⓓ	19.	Ⓐ Ⓑ Ⓒ Ⓓ
2.	Ⓐ Ⓑ Ⓒ Ⓓ	8.	Ⓐ Ⓑ Ⓒ Ⓓ	14.	Ⓐ Ⓑ Ⓒ Ⓓ	20.	Ⓐ Ⓑ Ⓒ Ⓓ
3.	Ⓐ Ⓑ Ⓒ Ⓓ	9.	Ⓐ Ⓑ Ⓒ Ⓓ	15.	Ⓐ Ⓑ Ⓒ Ⓓ		
4.	Ⓐ Ⓑ Ⓒ Ⓓ	10.	Ⓐ Ⓑ Ⓒ Ⓓ	16.	Ⓐ Ⓑ Ⓒ Ⓓ		
5.	Ⓐ Ⓑ Ⓒ Ⓓ	11.	Ⓐ Ⓑ Ⓒ Ⓓ	17.	Ⓐ Ⓑ Ⓒ Ⓓ		
6.	Ⓐ Ⓑ Ⓒ Ⓓ	12.	Ⓐ Ⓑ Ⓒ Ⓓ	18.	Ⓐ Ⓑ Ⓒ Ⓓ		

CHAPTER 11

NETWORKING

1. A network node that forward messages from one network to another is called ________
   (A) Gateway (B) Switch
   (C) Links (D) Downtime
2. Which of the following is a command which when typed will clean the DNS Cache stored in a local machine?
   (A) ipconfig/ cleandns
   (B) ipconfig/flushdns
   (C) ipclean/dns
   (D) ipflush/dns
3. Which of the following options will allow you to create wireless PAN?
   (A) Firewire (B) Bluetooth
   (C) Infrared
   (D) Both (B) and (C)
4. For which of the following purpose DSL is used?
   (A) To encrypt data before forwarding.
   (B) To set a port for incoming mails.
   (C) To transfer digital signals over standard telephone lines.
   (D) Both (A) and (B)
5. A router ________ .
   (A) Makes sure that data sent over the internet goes to the right destination
   (B) Acts like a traffic controller - cuts down congestion and keeps data flowing smoothly along the best possible path
   (C) Both (A) and (B)
   (D) None of these
6. When internet traffic gets congested, routers ________ .
   (A) Re-route traffic to less congested areas
   (B) Focus on speeding up areas experiencing high-volume traffic
   (C) Trim data to ensure timely delivery despite congestion
   (D) All of these
7. Network cables that are used to connect a computer to a hub or switch is called ________ .
   (A) Patch Cable (B) Axial Cable
   (C) Jack Cable (D) None of these
8. Which of the following types of connector is used for connecting NIC to hubs?
   (A) RJ-45 (B) Fiber optic
   (C) VGA (D) AGP
9. When a few similar configuration computers are networked together and they share resources amongst each other without any centralized system, which type of network architecture is then formed?
   (A) Client server network
   (B) MAN
   (C) Peer-to-Peer network
   (D) WAN
10. The time taken to pass a message from one node of network to other is called ________ .
    (A) Bandwidth (B) Semantic
    (C) Latency (D) Throughput
11. Based on data transmission speeds, the basic category of communication channels

are _________ .

(A) Narrowband (B) Voice-band
(C) Broadband (D) All of these

12. The default port number for SMTP is _________ .

(A) 21 (B) 22
(C) 28 (D) 25

13. Which of the following statements is NOT true about Optical Fibers?

(A) It can transmit large volumes of data at very high speed and long distances.
(B) It can turn at sharp corners.
(C) It increases security against unauthorized tampering of information.
(D) It enables transmission of both analog and digital signals.

14. Which of the following is the name of device that is used to regenerate the network signal?

(A) Router (B) Repeater
(C) Bridge (D) Switch

15. Select the odd one out.

(A) Infrared (B) Optical Fiber
(C) Bluetooth (D) Wi-Fi

Achievers Section (HOTS)

16. Identify the following:

– It connects several computers on a network.
– It receives and transmits the data in a network.
– It is capable of checking data packets as they are received.
– It also conserves network bandwidth while delivering the message.

(A) Modem (B) NIC
(C) Hub (D) Workstation

17. A ______ is a computer that you can control or work on *via* a network, to which a user does not have physical access.

(A) Remote computer
(B) Local computer
(C) Standalone computer
(D) Host computer

18. Which of the following statements is INCORRECT about IP address?

(A) It is a combination of numbers separated by dots.
(B) It can be either public or private.
(C) It is used to identify a computer on a TCP/IP network.
(D) An IPv4 address consists of a group of four numbers, from 1 to 255.

19. Which of the following is a network discovery technology developed by Apple Inc. that allows users to setup a network without any manual configuration?

(A) Bonjour (B) iConnect
(C) iZero (D) iConfiguration

20. Switches are preferred over hubs for networking because _________ .

(A) They give better network performance than hubs
(B) Bandwidth is shared in switches
(C) A switch generally costs less to purchase than a hub
(D) All of these

☺☺☺

Darken your choice with HB Pencil

1.	Ⓐ	Ⓑ	Ⓒ	Ⓓ	7.	Ⓐ	Ⓑ	Ⓒ	Ⓓ	13.	Ⓐ	Ⓑ	Ⓒ	Ⓓ	19.	Ⓐ	Ⓑ	Ⓒ	Ⓓ
2.	Ⓐ	Ⓑ	Ⓒ	Ⓓ	8.	Ⓐ	Ⓑ	Ⓒ	Ⓓ	14.	Ⓐ	Ⓑ	Ⓒ	Ⓓ	20.	Ⓐ	Ⓑ	Ⓒ	Ⓓ
3.	Ⓐ	Ⓑ	Ⓒ	Ⓓ	9.	Ⓐ	Ⓑ	Ⓒ	Ⓓ	15.	Ⓐ	Ⓑ	Ⓒ	Ⓓ					
4.	Ⓐ	Ⓑ	Ⓒ	Ⓓ	10.	Ⓐ	Ⓑ	Ⓒ	Ⓓ	16.	Ⓐ	Ⓑ	Ⓒ	Ⓓ					
5.	Ⓐ	Ⓑ	Ⓒ	Ⓓ	11.	Ⓐ	Ⓑ	Ⓒ	Ⓓ	17.	Ⓐ	Ⓑ	Ⓒ	Ⓓ					
6.	Ⓐ	Ⓑ	Ⓒ	Ⓓ	12.	Ⓐ	Ⓑ	Ⓒ	Ⓓ	18.	Ⓐ	Ⓑ	Ⓒ	Ⓓ					

CHAPTER 12

LATEST DEVELOPMENTS IN THE FIELD OF IT

1. Which of the following animated movie is produced by Pixar Animation Studios?
   (A) Frozen
   (B) The Jungle Book
   (C) Finding Dory
   (D) Minions
2. Which of the following is an online multiplayer gaming and digital media service for Xbox One?
   (A) Xbox station (B) Xbox shipping
   (C) Xbox Live (D) Xbox Digital
3. Convertible laptops falls in the category of _____ laptops.
   (A) Analog (B) Hybrid
   (C) Stationary (D) Traditional
4. _____ display is an emerging technology in IT that will display the information by directly projecting images onto the human retina.
   (A) Screenless (B) Touch Screen
   (C) Retina (D) Haptic
5. Which of the following is a feature of body-borne computers?
   (A) Constant interaction
   (B) Multi-tasking
   (C) User-friendly interface
   (D) All of these
6. HMDs are devices that are used in virtual reality or aviation applications to project an imaginary scene as real scene. HMD is an acronym of ________ .
   (A) Heavy Metal Display
   (B) Head Mounted Display
   (C) Heavy Molded Display
   (D) Home Mode Display
7. What do you mean by power bank?
   (A) A mobile app that let you store your photos and videos.
   (B) A telecommunication service to make free phone calls.
   (C) A security feature for smartphones.
   (D) A device that provides energy to mobile devices.
8. __________ is known as the predecessor of 'Wikipedia'.
   (A) Nupedia (B) Cyclopedia
   (C) Infopedia (D) None of these
9. Live television, Video on Demand and time shifted television are services offered by ________.
   (A) IPTV (B) HTTV
   (C) VOTP (D) Colde TV
10. Google Now, an intelligent personal assistant by Google can provide ________.
    (A) Weather Information
    (B) Sports Updates (C) Nearby Events
    (D) All of these
11. _______ is a downloadable image recognition application by Google.
    (A) Google Images (B) Google Movies
    (C) Google Goggles (D) Google Video
12. Additive manufacturing is the term used to refer _______ .
    (A) 3D Printing (B) Data Mining

(C) Artificial Intelligence
(D) Concept Manufacturing

13. A data storage technology developed by Apple Inc. that combines the performance of Flash storage and hard disk drive is known as _____.
(A) Compound Drive
(B) iMerge Drive
(C) Fusion Drive
(D) iStorage Drive

14. Computer system that uses natural language processing and machine learning to enable people and machines to interact naturally with the environment are called ________ system .
(A) Holographic (B) Fusion
(C) Compound (D) Cognitive

15. Which of the following statements hold(s) true about smartwatch?
Statement 1 : It may include features such as GPS navigation and touchscreen.
Statement 2 : It may support wireless technologies like Wi-Fi and Bluetooth.
(A) Only Statement 1
(B) Only Statement 2
(C) Both Statement 1 and Statement 2
(D) Neither Statement 1 nor Statement 2

16. Which of the following technology is used for identifying and capturing data automatically?
(A) RFID
(B) Voice Recognition
(C) OCR
(D) All of these

17. A robot designed to look and act like a human.
(A) Humroid (B) Android
(C) Dendroid (D) Hrobo

18. Select odd one out.
(A) (B)
(C) (D)

19. What is the name of biometric security system of Windows 10, that let user sign-in to a computer through recognizing his face or fingerprints?
(A) Windows To Go (B) Windows Hello
(C) Windows Bio (D) Windows Scan

20. Which of the following statements hold(s) true about machine vision?
Statement 1 : It is a technique used for automatic extraction of useful information by image capturing and analysis.
Statement 2 : It was introduced by Sundar Pichai.
(A) Only Statement 1
(B) Only Statement 2
(C) Both Statement 1 and Statement 2
(D) Neither Statement 1 nor Statement 2

☺☺☺

Darken your choice with HB Pencil

1.	Ⓐ Ⓑ Ⓒ Ⓓ	7.	Ⓐ Ⓑ Ⓒ Ⓓ	13.	Ⓐ Ⓑ Ⓒ Ⓓ	19.	Ⓐ Ⓑ Ⓒ Ⓓ
2.	Ⓐ Ⓑ Ⓒ Ⓓ	8.	Ⓐ Ⓑ Ⓒ Ⓓ	14.	Ⓐ Ⓑ Ⓒ Ⓓ	20.	Ⓐ Ⓑ Ⓒ Ⓓ
3.	Ⓐ Ⓑ Ⓒ Ⓓ	9.	Ⓐ Ⓑ Ⓒ Ⓓ	15.	Ⓐ Ⓑ Ⓒ Ⓓ		
4.	Ⓐ Ⓑ Ⓒ Ⓓ	10.	Ⓐ Ⓑ Ⓒ Ⓓ	16.	Ⓐ Ⓑ Ⓒ Ⓓ		
5.	Ⓐ Ⓑ Ⓒ Ⓓ	11.	Ⓐ Ⓑ Ⓒ Ⓓ	17.	Ⓐ Ⓑ Ⓒ Ⓓ		
6.	Ⓐ Ⓑ Ⓒ Ⓓ	12.	Ⓐ Ⓑ Ⓒ Ⓓ	18.	Ⓐ Ⓑ Ⓒ Ⓓ		

LOGICAL REASONING

VERBAL REASONING

1. Introducing a man, a woman says, "His wife is the only daughter of my father". How is the man related to the woman?
(A) Brother (B) Father-in-law
(C) Husband (D) Paternal uncle

2. Harsh Jain has three children – Sunita, Ravi and Arun. Arun married Rashi, the eldest daughter of Mr and Mrs Mittal. The Mittal's married their youngest daughter to the eldest son of Mr and Mrs Sharma and they had two children named Manish and Priya. The Mittal's have two more children, Anuj and Neha, both elder to Vanshika. Sameer and Ajay are sons of Arun and Rashi. Rashmi is the daughter of Manish. What is the surname of Rashmi?
(A) Sharma (B) Mittal
(C) Jain (D) None of these

3. In a row of girls, Sonam and Anita occupy the ninth place from the right end and tenth place from the left end respectively. If they interchange their places, then Sonam occupies seventeenth place from the right end. How many girls are there in the row?
(A) 25
(B) 26
(C) 27
(D) Data inadequate

4. Find the missing number, if same rule is followed in all the three figures.

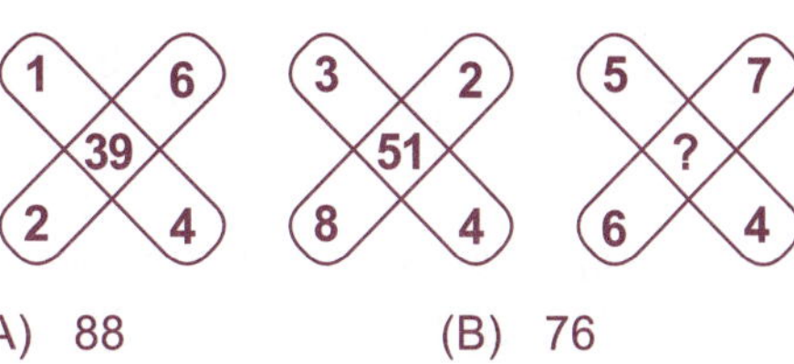

(A) 88 (B) 76
(C) 92 (D) 80

Direction (5-6) : In each of the following questions, two rows of numbers are given. The resultant number in each row is to be worked out separately based on the following rules and the questions below the rows of numbers are to be answered. The operations on numbers progress from left to right.

Rules:

(i) If an odd number is followed by another composite odd number, they are to be added.
(ii) If an even number is followed by an odd number, they are to be added.
(iii) If an even number is followed by a number which is the perfect square, the even number is to be subtracted from the perfect square.
(iv) If an odd number is followed by a prime odd number, the first number is to be divided by the second number.
(v) If an odd number is followed by an even number, the second one is to be subtracted from the first number.

5. 15 8 21
p 3 27
If p is the resultant of the first row, what will be the resultant of the second row?
(A) 58 (B) 76
(C) 27 (D) 82

6. 12 64 17
20 69 16
If m, n are the resultants of the first and second row respectively, then find $\frac{n-m}{2}$.
(A) 24 (B) 2
(C) $\frac{5}{2}$ (D) $\frac{3}{2}$

7. In the given number series, one term is wrong. Find out the wrong term.
5, 10, 17, 24, 37
(A) 10 (B) 17
(C) 24 (D) 37

8. In a certain code language, GEOPHYSICS is written as IOPDHZRJBT. How is ALTIMETERS written in that code language?
(A) NHULBFSDQT
(B) NIUKBFSDQT
(C) NHUKCFSDQT
(D) NHUKBFSFQT

9. There is a certain relationship between the pair of letters given on either side of : :. Identify the relationship of given pair and find the missing term.
U P : W N : : M M : ?
(A) O K (B) P K
(C) O O (D) P P

10. In the given Venn diagram, if rectangle represents the males; circle represents the urbans; square represents the educated and triangle represents the civil servants; then the number indicating the educated civil servants who are both males and urbans is ________ .

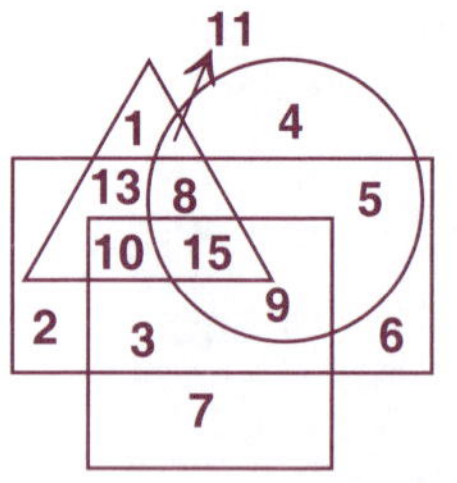

(A) 15 (B) 8
(C) 13 (D) 10

11. Five children take part in a tournament. Each one has to play with every other one. How many games they must play?
(A) 4 (B) 5
(C) 8 (D) 10

12. P and Q are brothers. R and S are sisters. P's son is S's brother. How is Q related to R?
(A) Father (B) Brother
(C) Grandfather (D) Uncle

13. Five students participated in the scholarship examination. Shobha scored more marks than Veena. Kavya scored lower than Rita but higher than Shobha. Meena scored between Veena and Shobha. Who scored least marks in the examination?
(A) Kavya (B) Veena
(C) Meena (D) Shobha

14. If $\rightarrow$ stands for 'addition', $\leftarrow$ stands for 'subtraction', $\uparrow$ stands for 'division', $\downarrow$ stands for 'multiplication', $\nearrow$ stands for 'equal to', then which of the following is correct?
(A) $2 \downarrow 4 \leftarrow 6 \rightarrow 2 \nearrow 6$
(B) $5 \rightarrow 7 \leftarrow 4 \uparrow 2 \nearrow 4$
(C) $3 \downarrow 6 \uparrow 2 \rightarrow 3 \leftarrow 6 \nearrow 6$
(D) $7 \leftarrow 4 \rightarrow 3 \uparrow 6 \downarrow 1 \nearrow 4$

15. I travelled 15 km Eastward and another 10 km Southward. I turned Westward and moved 10 km and again another 10 km Southward. A travel of another 5 km Westward and then 20 km Northward ended my journey. Identify the sketch depicting my journey.

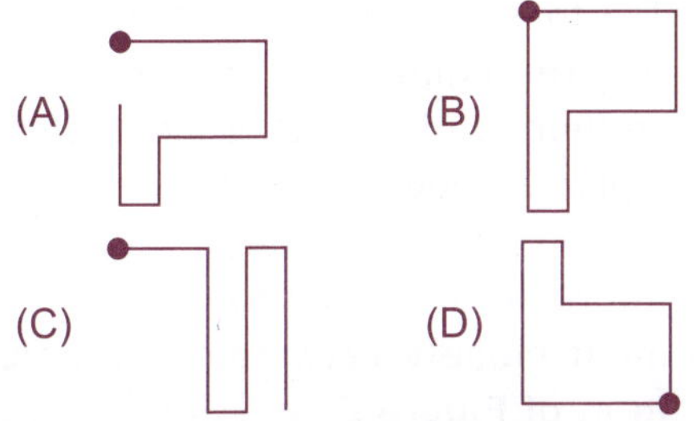

NON-VERBAL REASONING

16. Choose the option which most closely resembles the mirror image of the given combination, if the mirror is placed vertically to the right.

JAN24MON16

(A) 6ƖИOM4ƧИAᒐ (B) ᒐAИƧ4MOИƖ6
(C) 9ƖNOW42NAᒋ (D) 61NOM42NAJ

17. Select a figure from the options which completes the given figure matrix.

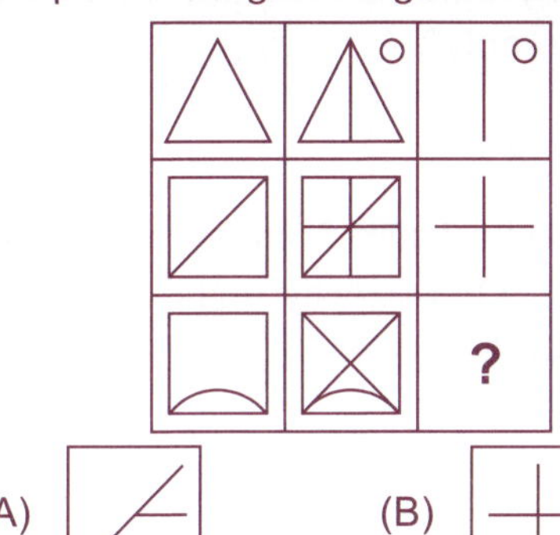

18. The three different positions of a dice are given below.

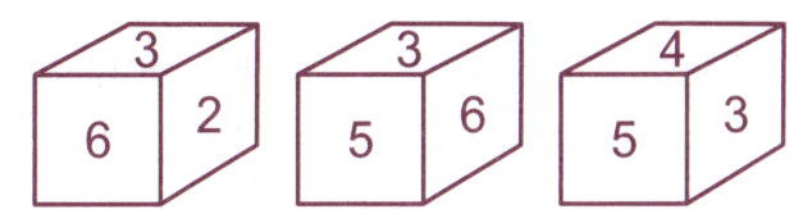

Which number occurs on the face opposite to the face having 1?

(A) 3 (B) 4
(C) 5 (D) 6

19. Select the figure from the options which does not satisfy the same conditions of placement of dots as in Fig. (X).

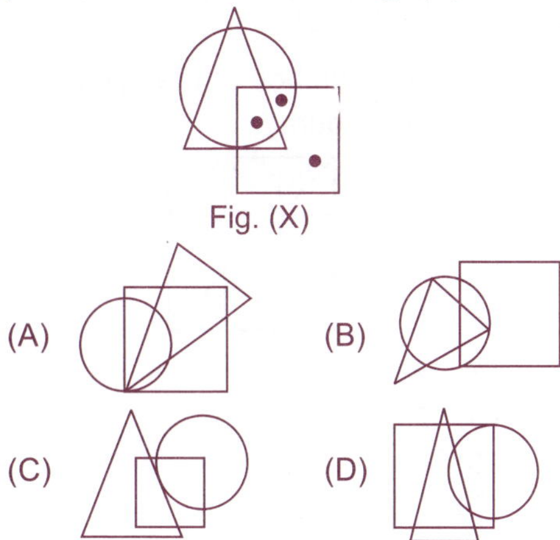

20. Which of the following options will continue the same series as established by the Problem Figures?

Problem Figures

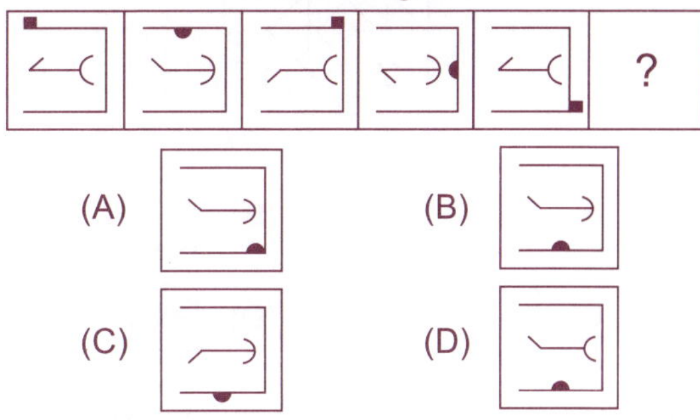

21. There is a certain relationship between the figures (i) and (ii). Establish the similar relationship between the figures (iii) and (iv) by selecting a suitable figure from the options which will replace the (?) in figure (iv).

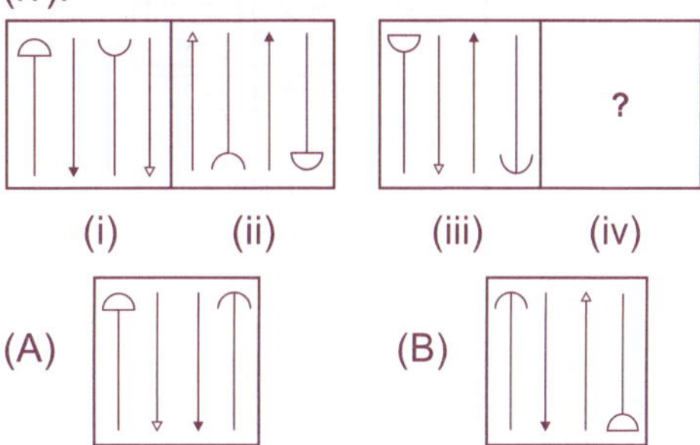

(C) 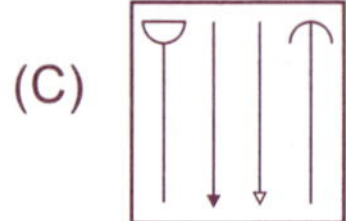 (D) 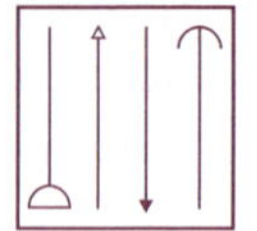

22. Find the number of triangles formed in the given figure.

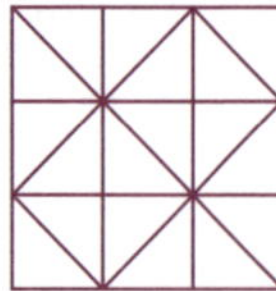

(A) 28
(B) 26
(C) 30
(D) None of these

23. Select a figure from the options which will complete the pattern given in Fig. (X).

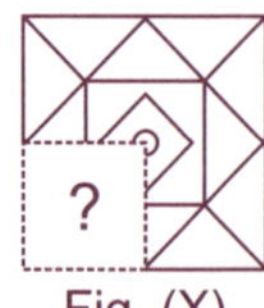

Fig. (X)

(A) (B)
(C) (D)

24. Group the given figures into three classes using each figure only once.

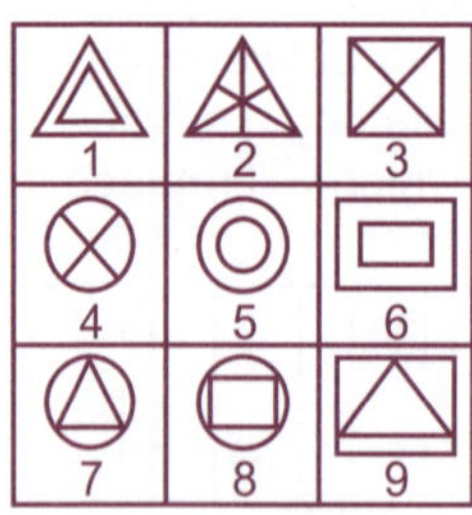

(A) 1,2,3 ; 4,5,8 ; 6,7,9
(B) 1,5,6 ; 2,3,4 ; 7,8,9
(C) 1,3,5 ; 2,4,8 ; 6,7,9
(D) 1,4,7 ; 2,5,8 ; 3,6,9

25. The following question consists of a set of three figures X, Y and Z showing a sequence of folding a piece of paper. Figure Z shows the manner in which the folded paper has been cut. Select a figure from the options which would most closely resemble the unfolded form of Figure Z.

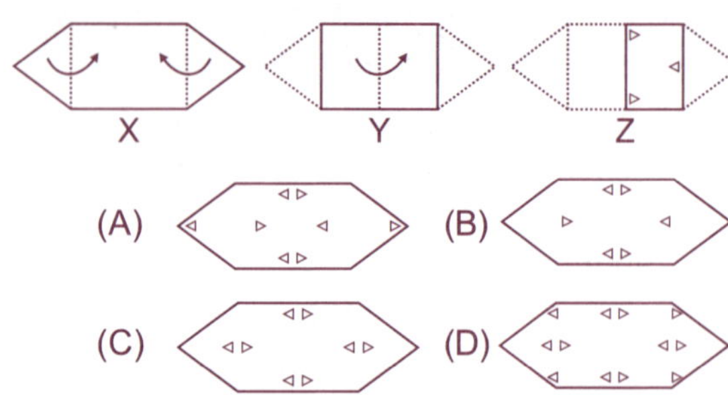

(A) (B)
(C) (D)

26. A cube, painted yellow on all faces and cut into 27 small cubes of equal size. How many small cubes are painted on one face only?

(A) 1 (B) 6
(C) 8 (D) 12

27. Select a figure from the options in which Fig. (X) is exactly embedded as one of its part.

Fig. (X)

(A) (B)
(C) (D)

28. Select the pair from the options that has a relationship similar to that in the given pair.

(A) 

(B)

(C) 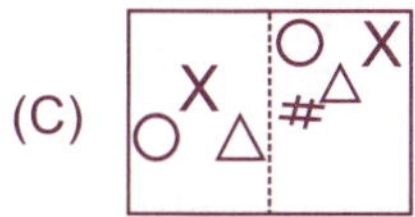

(D) 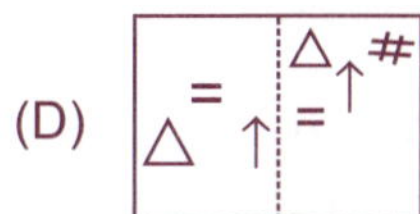

29. Which of the following options will replace the question mark in the given figure matrix?

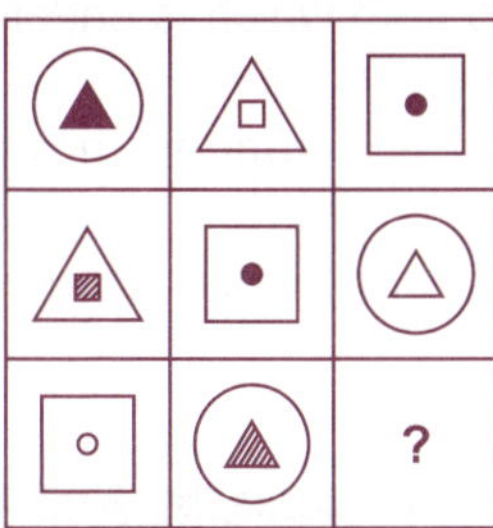

(A) 

(B) 

(C) 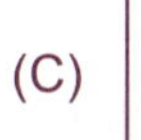 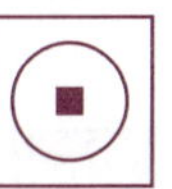

(D)

30. Choose the odd one out.

(A) 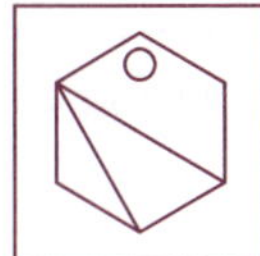

(B)  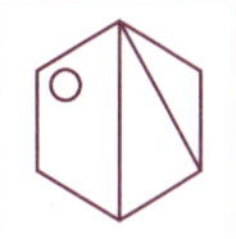

(C) 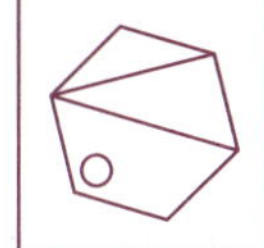

(D) 

☺☺☺

Darken your choice with HB Pencil

1.	Ⓐ	Ⓑ	Ⓒ	Ⓓ	9.	Ⓐ	Ⓑ	Ⓒ	Ⓓ	17.	Ⓐ	Ⓑ	Ⓒ	Ⓓ	25.	Ⓐ	Ⓑ	Ⓒ	Ⓓ
2.	Ⓐ	Ⓑ	Ⓒ	Ⓓ	10.	Ⓐ	Ⓑ	Ⓒ	Ⓓ	18.	Ⓐ	Ⓑ	Ⓒ	Ⓓ	26.	Ⓐ	Ⓑ	Ⓒ	Ⓓ
3.	Ⓐ	Ⓑ	Ⓒ	Ⓓ	11.	Ⓐ	Ⓑ	Ⓒ	Ⓓ	19.	Ⓐ	Ⓑ	Ⓒ	Ⓓ	27.	Ⓐ	Ⓑ	Ⓒ	Ⓓ
4.	Ⓐ	Ⓑ	Ⓒ	Ⓓ	12.	Ⓐ	Ⓑ	Ⓒ	Ⓓ	20.	Ⓐ	Ⓑ	Ⓒ	Ⓓ	28.	Ⓐ	Ⓑ	Ⓒ	Ⓓ
5.	Ⓐ	Ⓑ	Ⓒ	Ⓓ	13.	Ⓐ	Ⓑ	Ⓒ	Ⓓ	21.	Ⓐ	Ⓑ	Ⓒ	Ⓓ	29.	Ⓐ	Ⓑ	Ⓒ	Ⓓ
6.	Ⓐ	Ⓑ	Ⓒ	Ⓓ	14.	Ⓐ	Ⓑ	Ⓒ	Ⓓ	22.	Ⓐ	Ⓑ	Ⓒ	Ⓓ	30.	Ⓐ	Ⓑ	Ⓒ	Ⓓ
7.	Ⓐ	Ⓑ	Ⓒ	Ⓓ	15.	Ⓐ	Ⓑ	Ⓒ	Ⓓ	23.	Ⓐ	Ⓑ	Ⓒ	Ⓓ					
8.	Ⓐ	Ⓑ	Ⓒ	Ⓓ	16.	Ⓐ	Ⓑ	Ⓒ	Ⓓ	24.	Ⓐ	Ⓑ	Ⓒ	Ⓓ					

HINTS & EXPLANATIONS

1 Fundamentals of Computer

1. (C) : A processor register is a very fast computer memory used to speed the execution of computer programs by providing quick access to commonly used values.

2. (C) **3. (B)**

4. (A) : Graphical User Interface enables a user to interact with a computer system using items such as icons, windows, pointers, etc.

5. (A) **6. (D)**

7. (A) : SD card is a non-volatile memory card. So, only statement 1 is true.

8. (D)

9. (C) : CMOS is a small battery that stores the BIOS settings. This information ranges from the system time and date to system hardware settings for your computer.

10. (D) **11. (D)** **12. (C)**

13. (A) : Flash CS6 is used for producing animation for games, internet applications, etc.

14. (C) **15. (D)**

16. (A) : A light pen is a pointing device, used to point select and draw on screen.

17. (B) **18. (A)** **19. (C)**

20. (C) : Among all options, Debian is an operating system which is a type of system software.

21. (B) : Worms, viruses, trojans, spyware, adware and rootkits, etc. are malicious software that can harm your computer.

22. (D) **23. (A)**

24. (D) : The given logo is of Snipping tool, which is a screenshot utility, so none of the statements mentioned in options (A), (B) and (C) is true.

25. (B) : Real time operating systems are quick respondent system that guarantees a certain capability within a specified time constraint.

26. (D) **27. (A)** **28. (C)**

29. (B) **30. (B)**

31. (B) : Language processors are programs which translate the program written in a programming language by the user into an executable program which is understood by the hardware of the computer.

32. (D) : SIMM is a random access memory module not sequential.

33. (B) : There is no such interface called as EDE.

34. (B) **35. (C)**

2 Algorithms and Flowcharts in Programming

1. (B) **2. (B)** **3. (D)**

4. (A) : Statements which sets or resets the value stored in a variable are called assignment statements.

5. (B) **6. (A)**

7. (A) : This symbol is used to indicate a process step or series of process flow steps that are formally defined elsewhere.

8. (C) **9. (D)**

10. (A) : Once a flowchart is drawn then it becomes cumbersome to modify it later on.

11. (A)

12. (C) : In flowcharts each symbol has specific meaning and context in which they can be used, so, we cannot use symbol of our choice, because then it would become difficult for other users to understand the context in which you have used symbols.

13. (A) **14. (B)** **15. (C)**

16. (A) : Suppose value of X =10 and Y=20

X=X+Y $\rightarrow$ X= 10+20=30

Y= X-Y $\rightarrow$ Y= 30-20=10

X=X-Y $\rightarrow$ X=30-10=20

Now X= 20 and Y= 10

17. (B) **18. (D)** **19. (B)**

20. (D) : For input output statements, parallelogram shape is used.

3 Animations & Multimedia

1. (B) : A green screen effect is used to superimpose anything or anyone into a photo or video. To apply this effect the background is covered with green scene.

2. (B) **3. (A)** **4. (B)**

5. (A) : In interactive media the user can control the interaction with media elements. Similar while chatting, user can decide what to type, to whom it should be sent, etc.

6. (A)

7. (B) : A zoomable user interface is an interface that lets the user scale the viewable area.

8. (A) **9. (C)** **10. (A)**

11. (B)

12. (D) : In cycle animation a series of frames or illustrations is drawn in sequence, and then they loop to create an animation.

13. (C) **14. (A)** **15. (D)**

16. (C)

17. (C) : Rich media includes advanced features like audio, video and animations that appeal users to interact with the content.

18. (A) **19. (A)** **20. (C)**

4 Flash CS6

1. (B) : Adobe flash is proprietary software. It is available free for trial but only for a short period of time. So, it cannot be considered as free software.

2. (D)

3. (B) : To publish a file in Flash, go to File tab and select Publish operation.

4. (A) : Bone tool is used in Flash to show inverse kinematics effect. It is also used to animate characters with legs and arms.

5. (A) **6. (C)** **7. (A)**

8. (D) : A motion tween can be eased in or eased out using the motion property inspector.

Ease In : The motion begins slowly, before gaining speed as time progresses.

Ease Out : The motion begins quickly, before losing speed as time progresses.

9. (B) **10. (C)** **11. (C)**

12. (C) **13. (D)**

14. (B) : Library is a repository of reusable graphics, animations, buttons, sounds, videos in a flash file.

15. (C) **16. (A)** **17. (B)**

18. (C)

19. (A) : After applying the Break Apart effect, the text would get broken into multiple text blocks as shown here:

20. (D)

5 Introduction to Visual Basic

1. (B) : Mod operator returns the remainder after division, so, the given arithmetic expression would evaluate as

$1 + 1 - 2 \rightarrow 0$

2. (B) **3. (A)**

4. (D) : Forms provide the windows that make up a Windows application. It allows the Visual Basic developer to create windows and layout controls (such as buttons, labels etc.) in those forms to provide the application's user interface.

5. (C) **6. (A)** **7. (B)**

8. (B) : Replace function returns a string in which a specified substring has been replaced with another string.

Syntax of this function is: Replace (string, find, replace[, start[, count[, compare]]])

9. (C)

10. (A) : The image given in option (A) is of PictureBox not of Image tool.

11. (A) **12. (A)** **13. (C)**

14. (D) : Given here is a statement that can be used to display a message box with Ok and Cancel buttons in visual basic application.

MsgBox "All the changes would be saved permanently", 4, "Confirm Changes"

15. (A) : Line 1 will generate an error because If condition must have Then or GoTo keyword.

16. (C) : To set the position of form on screen, enable the Form Layout window by going to View tab and click on Form Layout Window option or click on its icon available on standard toolbar. Then, run your program once and then drag the form thumbnail on the Form Layout window to change its position.

17. (A) **18. (D)** **19. (A)**

20. (A) : Int() returns the integer portion of a number.

Round() returns a number to specified number of decimal places.

Instr()returns the position of the first occurrence of one string within another.

Trim() truncate the space from both left and right side of a string.

6 HTML

1. (C) **2. (C)**

3. (C) : <li> tag is used for displaying an unordered list using bullets, when <ul> or <ol> tag is not used.

4. (B)

5. (A) : The syntax of img tag is : <img src= "url" alt="text">

Here url specifies the path where image is stored and alt specifies the alternate text for the image.

6. (D)

7. (A) : The text attribute specifies the color of the text in a document.

8. (A)

9. (D) : Both the statements are correct. In the option (B), target attribute is used, which specifies where the linked page shall get open.

10. (C) **11. (D)** **12. (D)**

13. (D) **14. (D)**

15. (B) : Image given here shows how text look with cellpadding.

Table without cellpadding:

Month	Savings
January	$100

Table with cellpadding:

Month	Savings
January	$100

16. (D) : Void, hsides and box are valid values of frame attribute.

17. (A) **18. (B)** **19. (A)**

20. (A)

7 MS-Word 2010

1. (B) : In Full screen reading view, editing is not permitted by default, you have to select Allow Typing option to permit editing.

2. (B) : Clicking on this icon adds a footnote in the document.

3. (A) **4. (A)** **5. (B)**

6. (D) : Track Changes feature when enabled mark all the changes made to the document.

7. (D) **8. (A)** **9. (C)**

10. (C) : Word's AutoRecover feature saves information after specified minutes. You can change the time interval by going to Word Options → Save → change the time in "Save AutoRecover information after every" field

11. (B) : Hyphenation option available in Page Setup group of Page Layout tab allow Word to break lines between the syllables of words

12. (A) **13. (C)** **14. (D)**

15. (D)

16. (C) : Insert and link option insert the image in the word document and link it to the source file.

17. (B)

18. (A) : To embed fonts, go to Word Options → Save → Check the "Embed fonts in the file" checkbox.

19. (A) **20. (A)**

8 MS-Excel 2010

1. (A) : Absolute reference is used to keep a row and/or column constant, because they do not change when copied or filled.

2. (A) : To display a drop-down list for a specific range of cells, select Data Validation option and select List in Allow field of Settings tab in Data Validation dialog box.

3. (D) **4. (A)**

5. (B) : Trace precedents option when enabled show arrows that indicate what cells affect the value of currently selected cells.

6. **(C) :** To divide a worksheet into multiple resizable pane, firstly select the cell from which you want to divide the worksheet and then click on Split option in View tab.

7. **(C)** 8. **(A)**

9. **(B) :** Protect sheet feature does not protect the entire workbook, so only statement 2 is true.

10. **(B)** 11. **(C)** 12. **(C)**

13. **(B)**

14. **(A) :** The given image is of Subtotal icon, it is found in Outline group of Data tab.

15. **(D)** 16. **(D)**

17. **(B) :** Consolidate option combines values from multiple ranges into one.

18. **(B)**

19. **(B) :** To display a message when unwanted data is entered in a cell, select the range of cells, then go to Data Validation option, select Error Alert tab and type error message and click on OK button.

20. **(B)**

9 MS-PowerPoint 2010

1. **(D)**

2. **(A) :** Set Up Slide Show option is used to set up the tasks mentioned in the question.

3. **(C)** 4. **(C)**

5. **(C) :** Using Trigger, one can set a special start condition for an animation.

6. **(C)**

7. **(D) :** AutoFit Text to Placeholder option is available in AutoFit option, that gets displayed when a large block of text is inserted.

8. **(A)** 9. **(B)** 10. **(B)**

11. **(D)**

12. **(C) :** The icon shown in option (C)is used to show markup.

13. **(B)** 14. **(C)**

15. **(D) :** The icon shown in the question is of Mark Final option. So, none of the statements is true.

16. **(B)**

17. **(B) :** Publish slides option is used for this purpose.

18. **(A)** 19. **(A)** 20. **(C)**

10 Internet and Viruses

1. **(A)**

2. **(D) :** Malware programs are specifically designed to disrupt, damage, or gain authorized access to a computer system.

3. **(A)** 4. **(B)** 5. **(A)**

6. **(A) :** Pharming is the technique of directing a user to a website that mimics the appearance of a legitimate one.

7. **(A)** 8. **(D)** 9. **(A)**

10. **(A)** 11. **(C)**

12. **(C) :** It converts digital signal into analog signals and analog signals to digital.

13. **(D) :** A blog is a website consisting of entries appearing in reverse chronological order with the most recent entry appearing first.

14. **(B)** 15. **(A)** 16. **(D)**

17. **(D)** 18. **(A)** 19. **(A)**

20. **(A)**

11 Networking

1. **(A) :** Gateway is basically defined as a node on a network that serves as an entrance to another network.

2. **(B) :** DNS cache stores the locations of web servers that contain web pages which you have recently viewed. When the ipconfig/flushdns command is executed successfully the system returns the following message:
Windows IP configuration successfully flushed the DNS Resolver Cache.

3. **(D)**

4. **(C) :** DSL is a high speed bandwidth connection used to transfer digital signals over standard telephone lines.

5. **(C)** 6. **(A)** 7. **(A)**

8. **(A) :** RJ-45 is a connector used commonly to connect computers onto a local-area network (LAN).

9. **(C)**

10. **(C) :** Latency defines how much time it takes for a packet of data to get from one designated point to another.

11. **(D)** 12. **(D)** 13. **(B)**

14. (B)

15. (B) : Except option (B), rest all are wireless communication mediums.

16. (C) **17. (A)**

18. (D) : An IPv4 address consist of a group of four numbers, from 0 to 255.

19. (A)

20. (A) : A switch is preferred over a hub because a switch will only send message to device that needs or request it.

12 Latest Developments in the Field of IT

1. (C) **2. (C)**

3. (B) : A convertible laptop is any type of portable laptop that can essentially function as either a laptop or a tablet computer.

4. (A) : The screenless display technology is used to transfer or display information without using a screen.

5. (D) **6. (B)** **7. (D)**

8. (A)

9. (A) : IPTV transmits and broadcasts television programs through the Internet using Internet Protocol.

10. (D) **11. (C)**

12. (A) : It is called additive manufacturing because in an additive process an object is created by laying down successive layers of material until the object is created.

13. (C) **14. (D)** **15. (C)**

16. (D) **17. (B)**

18. (D) : Except (D), all are music apps.

19. (B) : It is a biometric identity and access control feature that supports fingerprint scanners, iris scanners and facial recognition technology on devices running Windows 10.

20. (A)

Logical Reasoning

1. (C) : Only daughter of woman's father is woman itself. So man is the husband of the woman.

2. (A)

3. (B) : Before interchanging positions,
Sonam's place from right end = 9th
Anita's place from left end = 10th
After interchanging positions,
Sonam's place from right end = 17th
Also, Sonam's place from left end = 10th
∴ Total number of girls = 9 + 1(Sonam) + 16 = 26

4. (A) : The rule followed is,
$(2 + 6)^2 - (1 + 4)^2 = 8^2 - 5^2 = 39,$
$(8 + 2)^2 - (3 + 4)^2 = 10^2 - 7^2 = 51$
So, $(6 + 7)^2 - (5 + 4)^2 = 13^2 - 9^2 = \boxed{88}$

5. (A) : First row : 15 8 21
= 15 – 8 21
= 7 21
= 7 + 21 = 28

∴ $p = 28$

Second row : 28 3 27
= 28 + 3 27
= 31 27
= 31 + 27 = 58

6. (B) : First row : 12 64 17
= 64 – 12 17
= 52 17
= 52 + 17 = 69

Second row : 20 69 16
= 20 + 69 16
= 89 – 16 = 73

Therefore $m = 69$ and $n = 73$

$$\therefore \quad \text{Now } \frac{n-m}{2} = \frac{73-69}{2} = \frac{4}{2} = 2$$

7. (C) : The pattern is:

5 →(+5) 10 →(+7) 17 →(+9) $\boxed{26}$ →(+11) 37

8. (D) : The pattern is,

G E O P H | Y S I C S
Reverse ↓ | Same ↓
H P O E G | Y S I C S
+1 –1 +1 –1 +1 | +1 –1 +1 –1 +1
I O P D H | Z R J B T

Similarly,

A L T I M | E T E R S
Reverse ↓ | Same ↓
M I T L A | E T E R S
+1 –1 +1 –1 +1 | +1 –1 +1 –1 +1
N H U K B | F S F Q T

9. (A) : The relation is U $\xrightarrow{+2}$ W
P $\xrightarrow{-2}$ N

Similarly, $M \xrightarrow{+2} O$

$M \xrightarrow{-2} K$

10. (A) : 15 is common in all diagrams. So, 15 represents educated civil servants who are both males and urbans.

11. (D) : Total number of games they play,
= 4 + 3 + 2 + 1 = 10

12. (D) : P's son is S's brother. So R is the daughter of P. Hence, Q is uncle of R.

13. (B) : Descending order of students according to their scores is

Rita, Kavya, Shobha, Meena, Veena.

Hence, Veena scored least marks in the examination.

14. (C) : (A) $2 \times 4 - 6 + 2 = 6$
$\Rightarrow 8 - 6 + 2 = 6$
$\Rightarrow 4 = 6$ (Incorrect)

(B) $5 + 7 - 4 \div 2 = 4$
$\Rightarrow 5 + 7 - 2 = 4$
$\Rightarrow 10 = 4$ (Incorrect)

(C) $3 \times 6 \div 2 + 3 - 6 = 6$
$\Rightarrow 3 \times 3 + 3 - 6 = 6$
$\Rightarrow 9 + 3 - 6 = 6$
$\Rightarrow 6 = 6$ (Correct)

(D) $7 - 4 + 3 \div 6 \times 1 = 4$
$\Rightarrow 7 - 4 + 0.5 = 4$
$\Rightarrow 3.5 = 4$ (Incorrect)

15. (B)

16. (A) : JAN24MON16 | ƏƖNOMߤƧNAᒐ

Mirror

17. (D) : In each row, the uncommon part of first and second figure is the third figure.

18. (A) : Numbers on the opposite faces of the dice are (4, 6); (3, 1) and (2, 5).

19. (C) : (A)

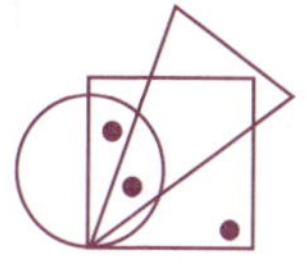

(B)

(C)

(D)

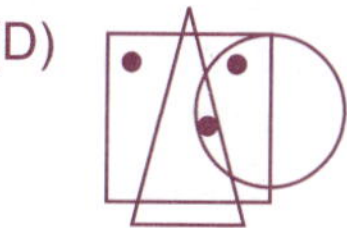

Hence, figure in option (C) does not satisfy the condition.

20. (B)

21. (B) : From figure (i) to (ii), every element gets inverted and element 1st, 4th & 2nd, 3rd interchanges their positions respectively.

22. (D) : Triangles formed are, A, B, C, D, E, F, G, H, I, J, K, L, M, N, O, P, Q, R, DE, EK, JK, JD, BC, AG, HI, NO, HN, IO, PQ, LR, AGBC, HIJD, BCDJ, AGHI, JKLR, IOPQ, OIJK, LRQP, XUV, XWV.

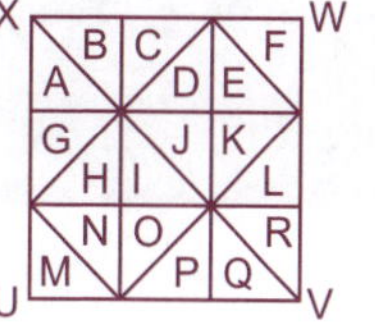

Total number of triangle formed = 40.

23. (A) :

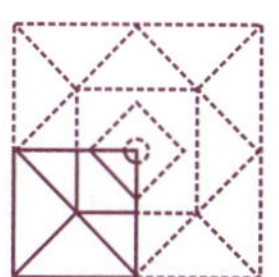

24. (B) : 1, 5, 6 have two similar figures one inside the other.

2, 3, 4 contains straight lines, each line divide the figure into two equal parts.

7, 8, 9 have two different figure one inside the other.

25. (C) :

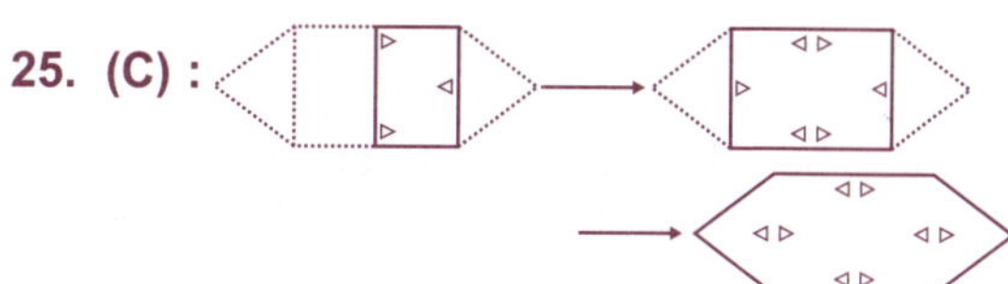

26. (B) : Number of faces only one face painted = 6

27. (C) :

28. (B) : From first part to second part, elements moves [figure] and new element add at the circled position.

29. (A) : In each column; every figure have two different element one is inside the other. Also one inside figure is shaded, one contains lines and one is unshaded.

30. (A) : Except figure in option (A), all are obtained by rotating each others.

☺☺☺

SOF NATIONAL CYBER OLYMPIAD

Each question in Achievers Section carries 3 marks whereas all other questions carry one mark each.

LOGICAL REASONING

1. Two rows of numbers are given. The resultant number in each row is to be worked out separately based on the following rules and the question below the rows of numbers is to be answered. The operations on numbers progress from left to right.

   Rules :

   (i) If an odd number is followed by another composite odd number, then they are to be added.

   (ii) If an even number is followed by an odd number, then they are to be added.

   (iii) If an even number is followed by a number which is the perfect square, then the even number is to be subtracted from the perfect square.

   (iv) If an odd number is followed by a prime odd number, then the first number is to be divided by the second number.

   (v) If an odd number is followed by an even number, then the second one is to be subtracted from the first number.

24	15	3
d	6	15

   If *d* is the resultant of the first row, then what will be the resultant of the second row?

   A. 37　　B. 8
   C. 22　　D. 29

2. Select the correct water image of given combination of letters and numbers.

   GRAPH923ICAL5

   A. ᘓʁ∀ԀH6ᘔƐIƆ∀⅂ϛ
   B. ƨ⅃AƆIƐƧ୧HꟼAЯᎮ
   C. ϛ⅂∀ƆIƐᘔ6HԀ∀ꓤ⅁
   D. ⅁⅂∀ƆIƐᘔ6HԀ∀ꓤϛ

3. Which of the following figures will complete the given figure matrix?

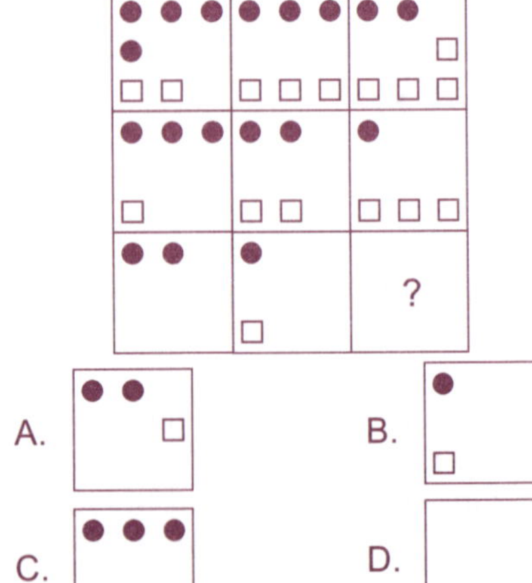

4. Nine friends A, B, C, D, E, F, G, H and I are sitting around a circle facing the centre. I sits 5th to the right of G. C is not an immediate neighbour of either G or I. B sits between H and E. C sits 4th to the left of E. D sits 2nd to the right of F. H is not an immediate neighbour of I. Who is 2nd to the right of B?

A. G
B. I
C. F
D. Can't say

5. Study the given Venn diagram carefully and answer the question that follows:

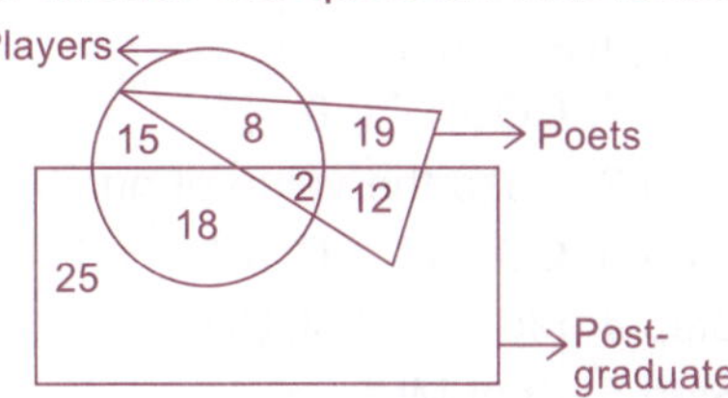

How many players are post-graduates but not poets?

A. 15
B. 2
C. 18
D. 8

6. Which of the following figures will continue the same series as established by the Problem Figures?

Problem Figures

A.
B.
C.
D.

7. If in a certain code language, 'SOLDIER' is written as 'SFJDKNR', then how will 'GENIOUS' be written in that code language?

A. FDMIPVT
B. TVPIMDF
C. FDMHNTR
D. HFOIPVT

8. Select a figure from the options which satisfies the same condition of placement of dots as in Fig. (X).

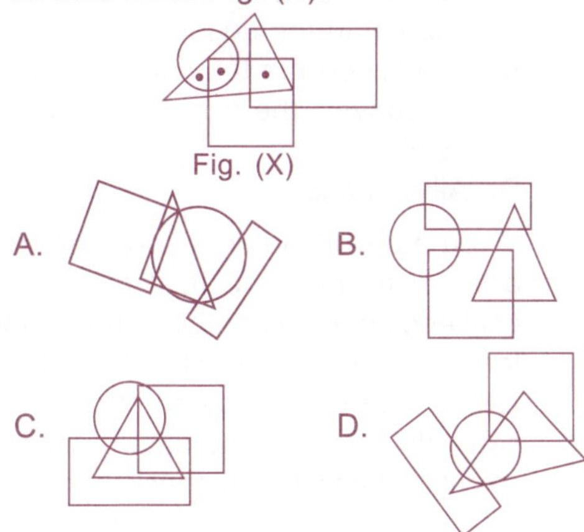

9. Puneet left his home for office in car. He drove 15 km straight towards North and then turned Eastwards and covered 8 km. He then turned to left and covered 1 km. He again turned left and drove for 20 km and reached office. How far and in which direction is his office from the home?

A. 21 km, West
B. 15 km, North-East
C. 20 km, North-West
D. 26 km, North-West

10. How many consonants are there in the given sequence which are immediately followed by a digit and immediately preceded by a symbol?

M N @ 1 T 2 # R U 3 © P Z K ★ 7 B A 6 £ G V 9 W 0 Y Z

A. None
B. One
C. Two
D. Three

COMPUTERS AND INFORMATION TECHNOLOGY

Direction (11-12) : Suppose you have added an auto text in the MS-Word 2010 document such that whenever you type word 'Goto' in the document, it is showing a text block (as shown in the image) and that text in the text block gets added in the document, if you press 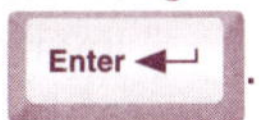.
Now answer the questions that follow:

Goto STEP 2 to repeat the proc...
(Press ENTER to Insert)
Goto

11. Which of the following features will enable you to add this auto text?

A. Quick Parts
B. Auto text parts
C. Auto text quick
D. Quick Auto text

12. What is the use of adding auto text to the document?
    A. To create, store and reuse pieces of content in the document
    B. To convert the text into wordart style
    C. To convert the text into equation or symbol
    D. All of these

13. If you are working on a spreadsheet with a lot of formulas in it, it may become challenging to comprehend how all those formulas relate to each other. Showing formulas in Excel instead of their results can help you track the data used in each calculation and quickly check your formulas for errors. Which of the following features of MS-Excel 2010 displays formulas in cells instead of their results right away?
    A. 
    B. 
    C. 
    D. Both A and B

14. Which of the following statements is CORRECT about the given icon of MS-PowerPoint 2010?

    A. It lets you to search text in the presentation.
    B. It lets you set the zoom level for the presentation.
    C. It lets you to add table in the presentation.
    D. Both A and B

15. Which of the following statements hold(s) true regarding the given icon of Visual Basic?

Statement 1 : It displays a text that the user cannot modify or interact with.

Statement 2 : It is known as TextBox.
    A. Only Statement 1
    B. Only Statement 2
    C. Both Statement 1 and Statement 2
    D. Neither Statement 1 nor Statement 2

16. What would be the result upon executing the given steps if the value of N = 3, in the given algorithm?

Step 1. COUNT = 0
Step 2. Read the value of number in N
Step 3. COUNT = COUNT + 1
Step 4. MUL = N*COUNT
Step 5. Print MUL
Step 6. Compare COUNT and 10
Step 7. If COUNT is less than 10 then repeat Steps 3 to 6

    A. 3 6 9 12 15 18 21 24 27 30
    B. 3 3 6 8 10 12 15 17 20 24
    C. 3 6 9 12 15 18 21 24 27 30 33
    D. 1 3 4 7 9 11 13 15 19 20 23 27

17. Match the following Visual Basic tools with their descriptions.

	Column-I	Column-II
(a)		(i) It is used to carry the specified action when the user chooses it.
(b)		(ii) It helps in resizing and moving an object.
(c)		(iii) It displays a list of items from which a user can select one.

    A. (a) - (ii), (b) - (i), (c) - (iii)
    B. (a) - (iii), (b) - (i), (c) - (ii)
    C. (a) - (ii), (b) - (iii), (c) - (i)
    D. (a) - (i), (b) - (ii), (c) - (iii)

18. The following criteria have been set in cell A1:
    - Data should be in text form only.
    - And, text length should be from 5 to 10.

Now, if user enters text anything excluding the mentioned criteria, then a message is displayed (as shown here) regarding invalid data. Which of the following features of MS-Excel 2010 will enable you to set your custom criteria in cells?

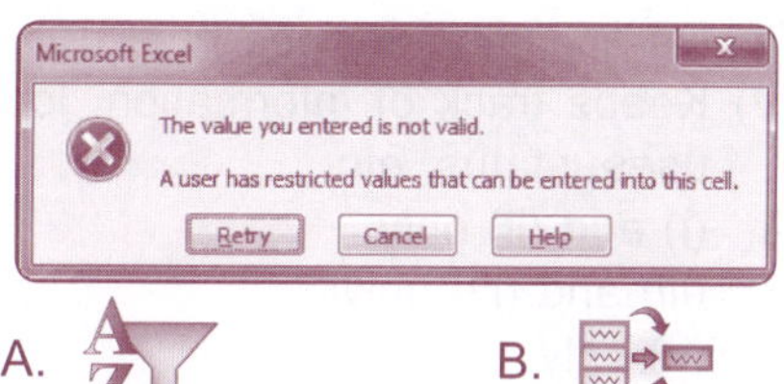

A. 
B. 
C. 
D. 

19. Which of the following terms is used for application software that is priced separately from hardware?
A. Unbundled
B. Unicode
C. Linker
D. Separator

20. Complete the given steps by replacing '?', if you want to disable certain default Windows Features in Windows 7.

Control Panel → ? → Turn Windows Features on or off

A. 
B. 
C. 
D. 

21. Identify the following:
– It is a protocol that is used to download an e-mail from the e-mail server.
– It is designed in a way that once you download the e-mail from the e-mail server, the mail is deleted from the server and then the protocol disconnects.
A. POP3
B. IMAP
C. FTP
D. NNTP

22. Which of the following statements is INCORRECT regarding the given topology?

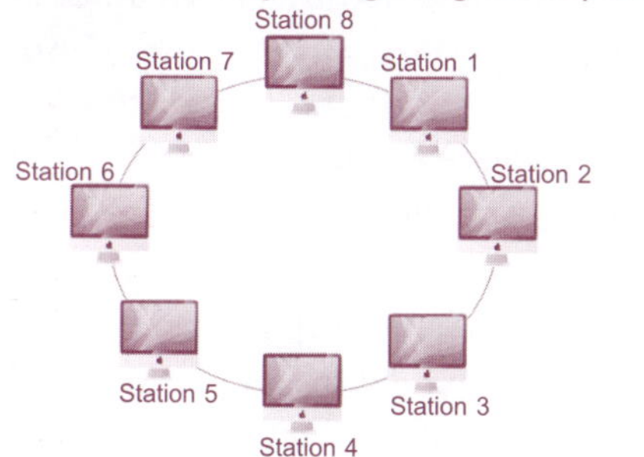

A. In this type of topology, adding or deleting a device requires changing any two connections.
B. A disabled station can disable the entire network.
C. It is known as Star topology.
D. Both A and B

23. Identify the following attribute of <a> tag in HTML, with the help of given description.
(1) The _______ specifies the URL of the page the link goes to.
(2) The _______ specifies the language of the linked document.
(3) The _______ specifies the relationship between the current document and the linked document.

	(1)	(2)	(3)
A.	href	hreflang	rel
B.	hreflang	href	relv
C.	href	lang	a-rel
D.	hreflang	lang	rel

24. Select the CORRECT match regarding Adobe Flash CS6.
A. – Binds two objects together
B. – Adds a new object to a group
C. – Adds a shadow effect to a button
D. – Used to add quick graphic patterns

25. What do you mean by the term mature technology?
A. It refers to the technology whose scientific background is well understood.
B. It refers to the technology whose modules is yet to be developed.
C. It refers to the technology that can be used by the scientist only.
D. All of these

26. Identify the following:
- It is an external storage hardware device developed by Data Robotics.
- It can connect to a computer using USB, Firewire port.
- It connects multiple drives into one external storage device that makes the data safe, no matter which hard disk fails.

A. Dropbox B. Drobo
C. Multi-Dro D. Disk-Drop

27. What is the name of biometric security system of Windows 10, that lets user sign-in to a computer through recognizing his face or fingerprints?
A. Windows To Go
B. Windows Hello
C. Windows Bio
D. Windows Scan

28. HMDs are devices that are used in virtual reality or aviation applications to project an imaginary scene as real scene. HMD is an acronym of ________ .
A. Heavy Metal Display
B. Head Mounted Display
C. Heavy Moulded Display
D. Home Mode Display

29. 1 byte can hold upto ________ of data and 1 KB can hold upto ________ of data.
A. 1 character, 2 or 3 paragraphs
B. 5 paragraphs, 1 character
C. 4 books, 1 character
D. 1100 MB Blu-ray disc, 1 character

30. Which of the following statements do(es) not represent the function of an operating system as a Device Management?
(i) Keeps the track of all devices.
(ii) Decides which process gets the device when and for how much time.
(iii) Allocates the device in the efficient way.
(iv) De-allocates devices.
(v) Keeps track of information, location, uses, status, etc.
A. (i) and (ii) only
B. (iii) and (iv) only
C. (v) only
D. (iv) and (v) only

31. In the given Visual Basic code, what does the statement return?
```
Private Sub Command 1_Click()
Print "Here it is" & Now()
End Sub
```
A. It returns the current system date and time.
B. It returns the current system time only.
C. It returns the current system date only.
D. It shows an error message.

32. Select the INCORRECT match regarding the Visual Basic code with their results.
A. Print Rtrim (" Oly ") + "2017" – Oly2017
B. Print instr ("Perform", "f ") – 4
C. Print Right ("Hello", 4) – llo
D. Print Mid ("Statement", 2, 3) – tat

33. The given image shows the Trace Precedents in MS-Excel 2010. Cell B1 contains the formula =A1*A2. What do exactly these arrows indicate?

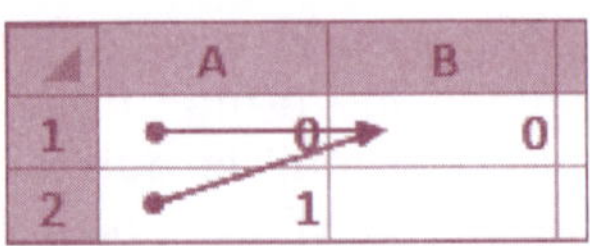

A. They indicate that cells A1 and A2 affect the value of cell B1.
B. They indicate that cells A1 and A2 are affected by the value of cell B1.
C. They indicate that the value of cell B1 is independent of the values of cells A1 and A2.
D. All of these

34. Whenever you are trying to edit a cell in worksheet of MS-Excel 2010, a message is displayed (as shown in the image), that makes you unable to edit the cell.

Complete the given step by replacing "?" to make that locked cell editable again.

Microsoft Excel

The cell or chart that you are trying to change is protected and therefore read-only.

Review tab → Changes group → ? → Type the password (that you had set while locking the cell) to unprotect sheet in "Unprotect Sheet" dialog box

A. Unprotect Sheet
B. Lock Sheet
C. Lock Cell
D. Unlock Sheet

35. Which of the following statements hold(s) true regarding Slide Master view in MS-PowerPoint 2010?

Statement 1 : In this view, you are only allowed to add pictures as placeholders.

Statement 2 : Slide Master is used in such situation, where you want to insert same logo in all slides.

A. Only Statement 1
B. Only Statement 2
C. Both Statement 1 and Statement 2
D. Neither Statement 1 nor Statement 2

36. Select the INCORRECT match regarding networking terminology with their descriptions.

A. Maximum Transfer Unit – The largest size data unit, a specific network can handle

B. Message Access Agent – A client-server program that pulls the stored e-mail messages

C. Teleconferencing – Audio and visual communication between remote users

D. Mesh topology – A network topology in which all computers are attached to a shared medium

37. You have created a presentation comprising of three slides. Which of the following sequence of slides will run in a slide show (after following the given constraints) when you select option in MS-PowerPoint 2010?

– Slide number 2 is hidden by using Hide Slide feature.
– Slide number 3 is highlighted in Slides Pane.

A. Slide 1 → Slide 2 → Slide 3
B. Slide 1 → Slide 3
C. Slide 3 → Slide 1
D. Slide 2 → Slide 3

38. Identify the following types of protocols referred as X and Y in the given statements.

– X is like Y because the data transferred between the client and the server looks like Y messages.
– Unlike Y, the X messages are not destined to be read by humans.
– Y messages are stored and forwarded, but X messages are delivered immediately.

A. X-HTTP, Y-NNTP
B. X-SMTP, Y-HTTP
C. X-HTTP, Y-SMTP
D. X-FTP, Y-HTTP

39. __________ is the process of finding and correcting program errors.

A. Debugging
B. Decoder
C. Demoduling
D. Phasing

40. Which of the following statements hold(s) true regarding Selection and Visibility pane of MS-Word 2010?

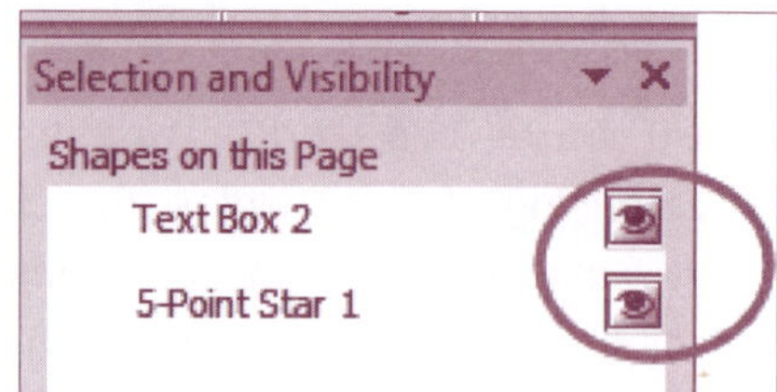

Statement 1 : It helps you to manage the inserted shapes, text boxes, SmartArt, images, or other objects in your document, like changing their order.

Statement 2 : Clicking on the eye shaped icons (marked by circle) will delete the objects from the document.

A. Only Statement 1
B. Only Statement 2
C. Both Statement 1 and Statement 2
D. Neither Statement 1 nor Statement 2

41. Which of the following technologies allows users to use applications without installation and access their personal fields at any computer with internet access?

A. 

B. 

C. 

D. dogpile

42. In which of the following areas, you can find the set of options shown in given image of Adobe Flash CS6?

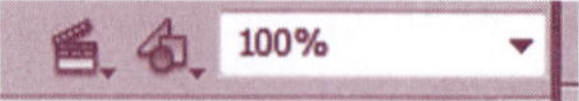

A. Stage
B. Timeline Window
C. Motion Editor
D. Tools Panel

43. To import elements on the stage, use the ________ key combination in Adobe Flash CS6.

A. 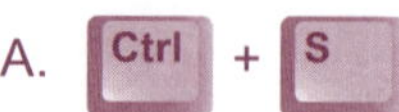

B. Ctrl + A

C. Ctrl + R

D. Ctrl + I

44. Typing wf.msc in search box of Start menu will ________ in windows 7.

A. Open Windows Firewall with Advanced Security
B. Open Control Panel window
C. Open Action Center window with Advanced Security
D. Open Taskbar Manager

45. What would be the output of the given HTML code?

```
<table rules="all">
  <tr>
    <th>Item</th>
    <th><del>Price</del></th>
  </tr>
  <tr>
    <td>Pen</td>
    <td>$10</td>
  </tr>
</table>
```

A.

Item	Price
Pen	$10

B.

Item	~~Price~~
Pen	$10

C.

~~**Item**~~	Price
~~**$10**~~	Pen

D.

Item	~~**Price**~~
Pen	$10

46. Identify the following feature of Windows 7.
    - It connects two computers so that one person can help troubleshoot or fix problems on the other person's computer.
    - It lets you open a direct connection between two machines over the Internet or over a Local Area Network. Even if you're hundreds or thousands of miles away, you can watch as the user demonstrates the problem and take control of the screen to make repairs quickly and accurately.

    A. Windows Remote Assistance
    B. Windows Demonstrate Assistance
    C. Windows Repair Assistance
    D. Windows Miles Assistance

47. Which of the following statement code of Visual Basic will display HEY 3 times?

    A.
```
Private sub command 1_click()
Dim var AS Integer
Var = 1
Do
   Print "HEY"
Loop while var <=3
End Sub
```
    B.
```
Private Sub Command 1_Click()
Dim Var AS Integer
Var = 1
Do
   Print "HEY"
   Var = Var + 1
Loop while var < = 3
End sub
```
    C.
```
Private sub command 1_Click()
Dim var AS Integer
Var = 1
Print "HEY"
   Loop while var = 3
   End sub
```
    D. Both A and B

48. The given snapshot appears when an installation program does not reach a successful conclusion. If an installation routine runs but fails for any reason to complete successfully (in some cases, even if you simply cancel out of the setup process), you will likely to see this message (shown here). What does this feature is known as in Windows 7?

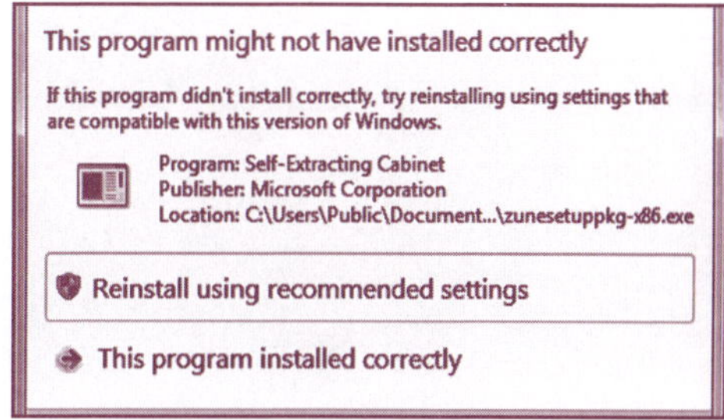

    A. Program Window Status
    B. Program Install Status
    C. Program Reinstall Assistant
    D. Program Compatibility Assistant

49. Suppose, there are two copies of the Word processor program loaded and the operating system treats each of these as a separate process. However, remember that there is only one processor, although there are several programs loaded into the main memory, the processor is actually processing one of the processes at one time. This ability to have more than one program concurrently loaded in the main memory is called _____.

    A. Multi user
    B. Multiprogramming
    C. Multitasking
    D. All of these

50. In networking, a protocol is a set of rules that govern data communications. The key elements of a protocol are syntax, semantics and timing. Which of the following key elements has been explained correctly below?
   (i) Syntax: Refers to the structure or format of the data, means the order in which they are presented.
   (ii) Semantics: Refers to the meaning of each section of bits, means how a particular pattern is to be interpreted, and what action is to be taken based on that interpretation.
   (iii) Timing : Means what data should be sent and how fast they can be sent.

A. (i) only
B. (ii) only
C. (iii) only
D. (i), (ii) and (iii)

☺☺☺

Darken your choice with HB Pencil

1.	Ⓐ Ⓑ Ⓒ Ⓓ	14.	Ⓐ Ⓑ Ⓒ Ⓓ	27.	Ⓐ Ⓑ Ⓒ Ⓓ	40.	Ⓐ Ⓑ Ⓒ Ⓓ
2.	Ⓐ Ⓑ Ⓒ Ⓓ	15.	Ⓐ Ⓑ Ⓒ Ⓓ	28.	Ⓐ Ⓑ Ⓒ Ⓓ	41.	Ⓐ Ⓑ Ⓒ Ⓓ
3.	Ⓐ Ⓑ Ⓒ Ⓓ	16.	Ⓐ Ⓑ Ⓒ Ⓓ	29.	Ⓐ Ⓑ Ⓒ Ⓓ	42.	Ⓐ Ⓑ Ⓒ Ⓓ
4.	Ⓐ Ⓑ Ⓒ Ⓓ	17.	Ⓐ Ⓑ Ⓒ Ⓓ	30.	Ⓐ Ⓑ Ⓒ Ⓓ	43.	Ⓐ Ⓑ Ⓒ Ⓓ
5.	Ⓐ Ⓑ Ⓒ Ⓓ	18.	Ⓐ Ⓑ Ⓒ Ⓓ	31.	Ⓐ Ⓑ Ⓒ Ⓓ	44.	Ⓐ Ⓑ Ⓒ Ⓓ
6.	Ⓐ Ⓑ Ⓒ Ⓓ	19.	Ⓐ Ⓑ Ⓒ Ⓓ	32.	Ⓐ Ⓑ Ⓒ Ⓓ	45.	Ⓐ Ⓑ Ⓒ Ⓓ
7.	Ⓐ Ⓑ Ⓒ Ⓓ	20.	Ⓐ Ⓑ Ⓒ Ⓓ	33.	Ⓐ Ⓑ Ⓒ Ⓓ	46.	Ⓐ Ⓑ Ⓒ Ⓓ
8.	Ⓐ Ⓑ Ⓒ Ⓓ	21.	Ⓐ Ⓑ Ⓒ Ⓓ	34.	Ⓐ Ⓑ Ⓒ Ⓓ	47.	Ⓐ Ⓑ Ⓒ Ⓓ
9.	Ⓐ Ⓑ Ⓒ Ⓓ	22.	Ⓐ Ⓑ Ⓒ Ⓓ	35.	Ⓐ Ⓑ Ⓒ Ⓓ	48.	Ⓐ Ⓑ Ⓒ Ⓓ
10.	Ⓐ Ⓑ Ⓒ Ⓓ	23.	Ⓐ Ⓑ Ⓒ Ⓓ	36.	Ⓐ Ⓑ Ⓒ Ⓓ	49.	Ⓐ Ⓑ Ⓒ Ⓓ
11.	Ⓐ Ⓑ Ⓒ Ⓓ	24.	Ⓐ Ⓑ Ⓒ Ⓓ	37.	Ⓐ Ⓑ Ⓒ Ⓓ	50.	Ⓐ Ⓑ Ⓒ Ⓓ
12.	Ⓐ Ⓑ Ⓒ Ⓓ	25.	Ⓐ Ⓑ Ⓒ Ⓓ	38.	Ⓐ Ⓑ Ⓒ Ⓓ		
13.	Ⓐ Ⓑ Ⓒ Ⓓ	26.	Ⓐ Ⓑ Ⓒ Ⓓ	39.	Ⓐ Ⓑ Ⓒ Ⓓ		

Hints & Explanations

1. (C) : Row 1: 24 15 3
= 24 + 15 3
= 39 ÷ 3 = 13

So, d = 13

Row 2 : 13 6 15
= 13 – 6 15
= 7 + 15
= 22

2. (A) : GRAPH923ICAL5 - - - - - - - - - - - - - - -Water level

3. (D) : In each row, the number of shaded circles are decreased by 1 and the number of squares are increased by 1.

4. (A) : The correct order of sitting arrangement is:

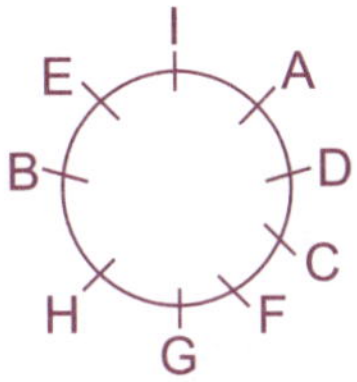

Clearly, G is 2nd to the right of B.

5. (C) **6. (A)**

7. (B) : We have, S O L D I E R

After reversing we get,

R E I D L O S

+1 +1 +1 ↓ –1 –1 –1

S F J D K N R

Similarly, G E N I O U S

After reversing we get,

S U O I N E G

+1 +1 +1 ↓ –1 –1 –1

T V P I M D F

8. (C) :

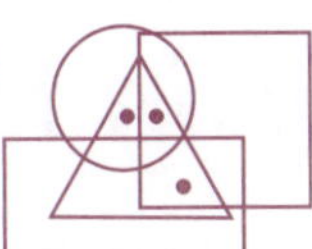

9. (C) :

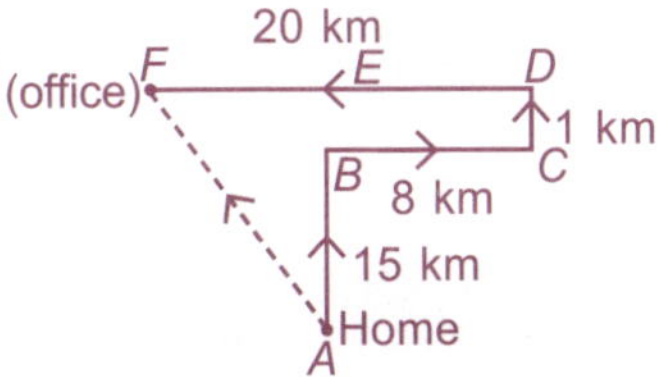

$AE = AB + EB = (15 + 1)$km = 16 km

$EF = DF – ED = (20 – 8)$km = 12 km

Now, $AF^2 = AE^2 + EF^2$

$\Rightarrow \quad AF^2 = (12)^2 + (16)^2$

$\Rightarrow \quad AF = \sqrt{256+144} = \sqrt{400} = 20$ km

Thus, Puneet office is 20 km in the North-West direction from his home.

10. (A)

11. (A) : To access this feature, go to:
Insert tab → Quick Parts in Text section → Click Auto Text option from the drop down menu.

12. (A)

13. (A) : Option (A) is the icon of "Show Formulas" feature that resides in Formulas tab.

14. (B) **15. (A)**

16. (A) : The given algorithm will produce the multiplication of number 3 as a result that is 3, 6, 9...30.

17. (A) : (a) is a pointer tool, used to move the object.

(b) is a command button, used to do the particular action when user clicks on it.

(c) is a list box, used to display a list of items from where user can choose one.

18. (C) : It is a Data Validation tool in Data tab used to prevent invalid data from being entered into cell.

19. (A) : Unbundling is the term used to dissemble the major components of the bundled software that usually accompanies OEM (Original Equipment Manufacturer) hardware.

20. (C) : Option (C) is of Programs and Features option of control panel.

21. (A)

22. (C) : The given image is of Ring topology. In a star topology, all computers are connected through central tool called as a hub or switch.

23. (A)

24. (D) : Option (A) - The lasso tool lets you create an irregular selection outline.
Option (B) - The Pen tool allows for point-to-point drawing, and precise control over curves and lines in between.
Option (C) - The 3D Rotation tool can be used on any movie clip instance to rotate and transform the symbol around x, y, and z axis.

Option (D) – The Deco tool is used to add graphic patterns instantly.

25. (A) **26. (B)**

27. (B)

28. (B) : It is a display device, worn on the head or as part of a helmet that has a small display optic in front of one or each eye.

29. (A) **30. (C)**

31. (A) : In Visual Basic, the Now () function is used to display the current date and time of computer system.

32. (C) : The Right () function returns a specified number of characters from the right side of a string.

The correct result of Option (C) will be ello.

33. (A) **34. (A)**

35. (B)

36. (D) : In mesh topology, every computer in the network has a connection to each of the other computers.

37. (B)

38. (C) : HTTP – Hyper Text Transfer Protocol, SMTP – Simple Mail Transfer Protocol

39. (A) : Option (A), Option (B) and Option (D) are not related to find and rectify errors in program code.

40. (A)

41. (A) : Option (A) is of Google Drive which allows users to store files in the cloud, synchronize files across devices, and share files.

42. (A)

43. (C) : Option (A) is used to save the current file in a particular folder / drive.

Option (B) is used to select all data.

Option (C) is used to import elements.

Option (D) is used to open the Info tab.

44. (A) **45. (D)**

46. (A) : To access this feature, go to:

Start → All Programs → Maintenance → Windows Remote Assistance

47. (B)

48. (D) : The Program Compatibility Assistant (PCA) runs in the background and monitors user initiated programs for known compatibility issues at run time. Whenever a potential issue with an application is detected, the PCA will prompt the user with pointers to recommended solutions.

49. (B)

50. (D)